The Music Lover's Library

GIOVANNI PIERLUIGI

DA PALESTRINA

PRINCIPE DELLA MUSICA

The Music Lover's Library

Choirs and Choral Music

By

Arthur Mees

Former Conductor of the Cincinnati May Festival Chorus;
Conductor of the New York Mendelssohn Glee Club,
of the Albany Music Festival Association, Etc.

With Portraits

GREENWOOD PRESS, PUBLISHERS
NEW YORK

Originally published in 1901
by Charles Scribner's Sons

First Greenwood Reprinting 1969

Library of Congress Catalogue Card Number 69-13995

SBN 8371-1967-7

PRINTED IN UNITED STATES OF AMERICA

TO

MY WIFE

Preface

AS chorus singing is the sphere of public
musical activity which now belongs legiti-
mately to amateurs, and choral music the class
of music for the performance of which the public is almost entirely dependent on amateurs,
the question as to how chorus singing and
choral music came to be what they are must
be of general interest. To throw light on this
subject is the purpose of this book. It is, therefore, not a compendium for the professional, but
a book for the amateur which will tell him
something about the beginnings and the course
of development of chorus singing; something
about the origin of choirs, their constitution,
and the nature of their activity at different periods; something about the history of the most
important choral forms, particularly the Mystery and the Oratorio, about their essential
characteristics, and about the first and other
notable performances of the best known of

them. In the chapter devoted to choral culture in America will be found a review of the conditions which led up to the organization of singing societies in this country, and of the circumstances under which the choral institutions that were conspicuously instrumental in elevating the standard of chorus singing were established. The last chapter is devoted to some observations on the qualities necessary to the efficient chorus singer and chorus conductor and on the general principles which, according to recognized authorities, should be observed in order to make choral performances what they ought to be.

If, in addition to giving information not within easy reach, this book—the first of its kind so far as the author knows—should succeed in demonstrating how puissant a factor in shaping the course of musical progress chorus singing has been in the past, and how necessary it is to the dissemination of sound musical taste at the present time, the author's purpose will be fully realized.

Contents

Portraits

Choirs and Choral Music

I

Among the Hebrews and Greeks

WHILE choral music was undoubtedly practised among the barbarous and uncivilised peoples from time immemorial in connection with the dance as an essential element of their religious ceremonies, it is to the music of the Hebrews and Greeks, the inheritors of the Egyptian and Assyrian theories, that the tone-art of the early Christians, out of which grew the tone-art of to-day, is directly traceable.

The highly imaginative and poetical spirit of the Hebrews, as illustrated in the eloquent epics and lyrics of the Bible, could not but seek vent in music, the art most intimately in accord with such a spirit and best adapted to satisfy it. It is not surprising therefore that the Hebrew tribes even during the nomadic existence which they led for many centuries — an existence ill calculated to encourage artistic activity—should have adopted and made serviceable to their own purposes such features

as appealed to them in the music of the peoples
with which they came into contact: the Assy-
rians and Egyptians. As national consciousness developed with concentration and a more
settled mode of life, the Hebrews found leisure
to transform and elaborate these elements in
accordance with their taste and the requirements of their religious observances, which
they delighted in investing with all possible
grandeur and impressiveness. To this end the
Levitic and prophet schools were instituted, in
which young men were instructed in arts and
sciences, music and poetry, in order to be fitted
for the duties which the state and the church
might demand of them. In these schools
bodies of instrumentalists and vocalists were
formed and made conversant with the poetic
and musical traditions, while those who gave
evidences of the creative faculty were entrusted
with the task of composing new poems and
melodies as occasion required.

The factors employed in the worship of the
Hebrews were, expressed in current terms,
soloists, selected choruses of men and women,
a grand chorus of the people, and an orchestra.
That this view is not a fanciful one is proven
by the biblical record and the fact that it is in
perfect accord with the spirit and the structure
of Hebrew poetry. The song of triumph of

4

Moses and Miriam after the destruction of Pharaoh and his host evidently enlisted the co-operation of such forces. The choirs chanted or sang antiphonally, the men responding to the intonation of Moses and the women to that of Miriam, while the multitude from time to time joined in refrains to the accompaniment of instruments, singers and players moving about in the measured steps of a panto-mimic dance. Whatever may have been the artistic merits of this celebration and similar ones, it is evident that the combination on a vast scale of music, poetry, and pantomime was calculated to produce a profound impression.

It remained for David, however, to place Hebrew tone-art on a firm basis. Possessed of extraordinary talent for poetry and music, which had been developed in the prophet schools, he realised that by investing the religious observances with pomp and magnificence he could create a feeling of national pride and political power which would prove of inestimable value to the future welfare of his people. He himself instituted the ceremonies amidst which the ark was brought to the tabernacle prepared for it, and appointed trained musicians to lead them and to have a care for their proper performance. These ceremonies are described in the First Book of the Chroni-

cles. A precentor gave out the chants and
conducted the choir of professional singers,
which was accompanied by harpers and players of the psalteries (probably a kind of lute,
the strings of which were plucked with a
plectrum). Three conductors kept the whole
body in time and in step by beating cymbals
as it executed the evolutions of a dance. The
trumpeters, who constituted a special division,
punctuated the different strophes or verses of
the songs with interludes adapted to the nature
of their instruments. David himself headed the
procession improvising at intervals in a rhapso-
dical manner words and melodies to the tones
of his harp, the chorus replying with refrains.

While the preparations for building the new
temple were in progress, David took measures
to increase the forces upon whom the performance of the service depended. The total number of singers and instrumentalists was raised
to four thousand, who were regularly instructed in the music of the ritual. Of these two
hundred and eighty-eight were masters of the
theory and practice of music, and these again
were subdivided into twenty-four classes, each
of which was under the leadership of one of
the sons of the three supervising Levites. On
extraordinary occasions choruses of women
and boys were permitted to take part in the

religious ceremonies, for the knowledge and practice of music were not confined to those set apart to officiate in the temple. Music was the common property of all classes and occupied a prominent place in private as well as in public celebrations. This David sanctioned and encouraged by attaching to his court a royal chapel, a trained chorus of men and women.

Solomon, David's son and successor, provided even more liberally for everything pertaining to the music of the temple and the royal household, in which he himself took an active part. The Song of Solomon, which was probably written for performance by the court singers, is supposed to have been a pastoral play imitative of a Hindoo idyl. As dramatic representations, however, were forbidden by law, it may have been given as a cantata by choruses singing antiphonally to pantomimic dances. That the poem is well adapted to such a treatment Palestrina illustrated by setting it to music in the shape of a choral dialogue.

The musical achievements of Solomon's reign reached their culmination in the services at the dedication of the newly built temple ; and on a scale of magnificence difficult to conceive these must have been if the record of Josephus is at all trustworthy. According to this historian the king commanded that for this great event as well as for permanent use thereafter two hundred thousand trumpets and trombones be constructed, and forty thousand stringed instruments, such as harps and psalteries, be fashioned of the finest brass, and that for the chorus of Levites two hundred thousand garments of fine linen be made. While this account is undoubtedly exaggerated it goes to prove that the ceremonies were of such grandeur as to give rise to extravagant estimates. The overpowering effect produced when "the trumpeters and singers were as one to make one sound" is eloquently described in II Chronicles, v. 13 and 14.

The temple service under Solomon marked the acme of the musical culture of the Hebrews, as Solomon's reign marked that of their political power. With the death of this great ruler the spirit of national unity disappeared, disintegration set in, and the religious ceremonies lost much of their dignity and splendor. A last attempt to restore them to their former estate was made by the Jews after their return to Jerusalem from the Babylonian captivity in 536 B.C., when they brought with them a trained choir of two hundred and forty-five men and women. With the destruction of Jerusalem by Titus, in 70 A.D., the remnants of the Jewish nation were dispersed, and what had been preserved by them of their original temple service was given over to the uncertainty of oral tradition. Thanks to the tenacity, however, with which the Hebrews clung to their religious ceremonies and customs, the scattered tribes retained essential features of their sacred art, which left their impress on the church music of the early Christians. This appears to have been the case particularly with the sect of the Therapeutæ, Essene Jews, who flourished in the neighborhood of Alexandria until the fourth century of the Christian era. The chants and hymns, old and newly composed, which they sang at their great religious festivals must have exerted a strong influence on the ritual of the Eastern Church, for to the initiative of the Therapeutæ is attributed the adoption by the Christians of antiphonal singing, the choral dialogue, which is undoubtedly of Hebrew origin, being a natural result of the antithetical character of Hebrew poetry.

While little is known regarding the musical system of the ancient Hebrews and regarding the melodies of their chants and hymns, there can be no doubt as to the lofty character of Hebrew music in view of the mission it was made to fulfil and in view of the exalted religious enthusiasm which permeates the poems to which it was wedded. Although it has been demonstrated, that the accent marks—not the vowel points, which are of much later origin—served as means of musical notation, the principle of deciphering them has not yet been discovered, and until this has been accomplished such ancient manuscripts as are still in existence are of little assistance in determining questions regarding Hebrew music. Nor can reliable conclusions be drawn from the services as now conducted in the synagogues, the songs or chants in use in the different countries of Europe, not to speak of Asia and Africa, having little in common. Nevertheless there are traceable in most of them certain intervallic progressions, embellishments, and cadences which are so characteristic and suggestive of Oriental music and are so evidently based on scales of their own as to justify the assumption that in them some of the elements of ancient Hebrew music have survived in spite of the unreliability of traditional transmission.

While the music of the Hebrews was calculated to impress by its grandeur and massive power, that of the Greeks depended for its effect on refinement and perfection of detail. The descriptions of Hebrew music which have been handed down, dwell principally on the external features of the musical celebrations. The treatises on Greek music, on the other hand, which have been preserved, are of a musico-philosophic nature and concern themselves with the most complicated problems in rhythm, metre, scale construction, modes, and with questions regarding the interrelation of music, poetry, and histrionics. True to their lofty views as to the mission of the tone-art, the Greeks evolved in the course of time a remarkably intricate and delicately constructed musical system, fitted to and corresponding with the forms of their epic, lyric, and dramatic poetry, on which it was based.

In Greek choral music, associated as it was with religious festivities, two distinct tendencies manifested themselves. The first of these had its origin in the worship of Apollo and was national and ethical in character; the second had for its source the cult of Dionysus, and was of an individual and sensual type. Within the former a large number of choral forms developed, such as hymns of praise, pæans of victory, prayers to Apollo, hymeneal songs, dirges and lamentations; the latter tendency was represented by one form only: the dithyramb, which Arion was supposed to have converted from a type of song used in Bacchic revels, into an antistrophic hymn. In this Greek tragedy had its source.

The festivals of Dionysus, the god of wine, were celebrated in the rural districts with orgies, processions, and games accompanied by dances to the strains of cyclic choric songs. According to tradition Thespis (600 B.C.) interlarded the strophes of these songs with the recital with pantomimic gestures of myths appertaining to Dionysus. By means of masks a single actor impersonated the different characters concerned in the narrative. In the course of time the recital was provided with instrumental accompaniment, and thus the melodrama was called into existence. Then, with the introduction of additional actors, the dialogue was made possible, and finally, with the employment of costumes, scenery, and stage mechanism, the apparatus of the Greek drama was rendered complete.

Each of these innovations necessarily tended towards forcing the chorus, which had originally been the main factor, into the background so far as its active participation in the play was concerned; yet the task which it was required to perform continued to be of the highest artistic significance and to demand the most thorough and careful preparation.

The place occupied by the chorus was the orchestra, a platform erected in front of and a little below the level of the stage, with which it was connected by steps, as at times the presence of the singers was required on the stage proper. With the action of the drama the chorus was not identified. Although composed of men only, it represented a body of men or women who, standing in no immediate relation to the characters in the play, annotated the occurrences with words of advice, warning, or comfort. At points of rest, between the scenes or acts, the chorus sang longer lyric pieces referring to the progress of the plot and its ethical purpose. In these *intermezzi*,—to use a familiar term—which were accompanied by appropriate gestures and most carefully designed evolutions, the full chorus, the chorus subdivided for the purpose of responsive effects, semi-choruses, and individual singers were employed. The chorus was kept in time and step and in accord with the instrumentalists by the corypheus, who marked the rhythm by clapping his hands, striking together pieces of wood or shell, or by stamping his feet, which were clad in sandals with wooden or metal soles so that the beats might be more distinctly heard. Such a conductor was subsequently called by the Romans *manuductor* if he made use of his hands, *pedicularius* if he made use of his feet.

In order to appreciate the importance of the dramatic representations in ancient Greece it must be remembered that they were not private undertakings intended for the amusement of the public, but festivals of a semi-religious character, which were considered essential to the political and moral welfare of the nation; that they provided the arena in which the master minds of the nation contended for supremacy, for the immortality of which the victor could be certain; and that they were therefore guarded in their every feature with jealous care. The rivalry which they stimulated extended to the choruses, for these were representative of the districts which furnished them, and to the successful one an artistically decorated tripod was awarded as prize.

The organisation of the choruses was provided for by law. The poet whose drama was to be performed made application for a chorus to a magistrate. If his request was granted, the best singers were sought out in each district and subjected to an examination. The requisite numbers having been selected, wealthy citizens chosen to be *choragi* furnished the means necessary for the sustenance, instruction, and equipment of the choir. The singers were then trained by a chorus master assisted by the leader of the orchestra, unless the poet himself preferred to assume this duty. The tripod presented to the best chorus became the property of its choragus, who dedicated it to a deity and placed it on a monument set up for the purpose. A street in Athens was completely lined with choragic monuments, of which one erected by Lysicrates about 335 B.C. is still in existence. The outlay for choruses was much increased in the course of time by the efforts of the choragi to make sure of the prize by securing professional singers and clothing them in the most costly and gorgeous costumes. It is related that one competitor expended ten thousand eight hundred drachmæ (about twenty-five hundred dollars) on choruses within two years, a sum which at the time was considered enormous. It was largely owing to the difficulty of finding choragi that the chorus was eliminated from the comedy.

While chorus singing was carefully nurtured in Greece in connection with the drama, it was likewise cultivated among the people as a valuable means of education and a refined type of diversion. The fact that the Greek philosophers devoted much thought to the question as to what modes or keys were best calculated to encourage strength of character and purity of mind, shows that music was held in honour as an important factor in the daily life of the people. Nor is it likely that the competitions in playing and singing which were inseparable from the numerous festivals of the Greek calendar, and which were listened to by the population of the whole country, should have failed to excite universal interest in choral music and to stimulate its practice. To choral culture among the people Archilochus (700 B.C.), the creator of the melodrama, gave artistic direction by inventing the iambics, which on account of their metre, corresponding to the flowing, graceful triple rhythm in music, and on account of their homely but spirited language appealed to public taste and called into life new folkmelodies.

Although the laws which governed rhythm and melody in Greek music are well known, no conception can be formed as to the manner in which they were applied in practice, for not a single well authenticated example of ancient Greek music has been preserved, unless the Hymn to Apollo found in the excavations at Delphi in 1893 be accepted as such a one. Whatever may have been the character of the music to which the monologues and dialogues in the drama, all of which were probably sung, were set, the fact that the choruses were invariably accompanied by dances gives colour to the assumption that they were of a rhythmically pronounced and easily comprehensible char-

16

acter, the rhythms being dictated by the pro-
sodic quantity of the syllables. While the
melodic rise and fall of the voice, according to
fixed cadences, was probably conditioned by
considerations of elocution, it conformed to
clearly recognisable intervals, in the acoustic
measurement of which the Greek theorists
were wonderfully expert.

It is all but certain that the chorus singing
was in unison, perhaps at times in octaves.
Into the instrumental accompaniment, however, melodies seem to have been independently introduced. These melodies were imitative of the vocal ones, and it was considered
very important that the answer to a given
theme—the counter theme—be constructed according to rule. It seems, therefore, that the
art of counterpoint, the art of consorting several individual melodies, was practised, in a
limited sense, by the Greeks.

The period of florescence of Greek music
created by the national enthusiasm and patriotic pride which followed the Persian wars,
was of comparatively short duration. Greek
music was not an independent art which could
thrive dissociated from poetry. When, therefore, about the middle of the fifth century B.C.
the decadence of the drama set in, music followed in its wake. Only in evolving theo-

retical systems on the basis of former artistic achievements important results continued to be accomplished. Although these systems could be on the whole of little practical value to the development of modern music—in certain ways they even retarded it—efforts were constantly made to apply them, under complete misapprehension of their purport, up to the sixth century of the Christian era.

The Romans, occupied with the extension of their empire and the establishment of their political power, contributed nothing towards musical progress. As singers and instrumentalists flocked to Rome from Greece there was no want of music, but only of music that pleased the vitiated taste of a people delighting in excesses and licentiousness. Choral performances were in great favour in Rome. It was Greek music however—Greek music of the popular kind, simple in rhythm and melody— which was sung on such occasions. In deference to prevailing custom these performances were conducted on the most elaborate scale. It is recorded that at the time of Julius Cæsar (100– 44 B.C.) twelve thousand singers and instrumentalists were gathered together in Rome to take part in a public celebration; and Nero (A.D. 37–68), who degraded the art by his ludicrous attempts at composing, singing, and playing, is said to have supported five hundred court musicians for his own entertainment. Ancient culture had run its course. Conditions were ripe for the spiritual and artistic revolution which Christianity effected.

II

In the Early Christian Church

FOR more than fifteen hundred years after
the dawn of the Christian era the practice
of music as an art was monopolised by the
Church; and as the Church discountenanced instrumental music, the history of choral music
during that long period is the history of music.
In the course of that time the most highly organised distinctively choral forms were invented and brought to a state of perfection by the
Church composers, whose sovereign command
of pure choral writing has never been surpassed
if it has been equalled. Instrumental music
however, upon which the tone-art depended for
further progress, and in which modern music
had its source, was left in the possession of the
people who followed the promptings of their
own fancy in spite of theoretical rules and notwithstanding ecclesiastical edicts.

While at the hand of the works of architect-
ure, sculpture, and painting that have been
preserved, it is possible to trace the course of

evolution of these arts under the influence of Christianity, there is little to be found, excepting fragments of theoretical and historical treatises, that might illustrate the development of music during the early centuries of the Christian era. Even if older manuscripts than those handed down — they are supposed to date from the eighth, possibly from the sixth century—should be discovered, little light would be thrown on the subject, for it was not until about the eleventh century that a system of notation came into use which indicated with any degree of accuracy the pitch and duration of tones, unless indeed the key for the methods of notation employed before that time has been lost. It seems reasonable, however, to assume that in music the primitive Christians, for a time at least, yielded to the same influences and were guided by the same practical considerations as in other matters pertaining to their religious observances.

It is a well known fact that social intercourse between Christian converts and pagans, so far as it did not offend religious beliefs and practices, remained unrestricted. In every-day life little difference was apparent between the customs and habits of the Christian layman and the Roman citizen. The buildings erected by the pagans, such as the Pantheon at Rome, the basilikas (halls of justice), and similar architectural monuments, were either turned into places of devotion or made to serve as models for such without a thought of the purposes for which they had been originally designed. In the catacombs, where in order to escape persecution the Christians were wont to assemble for exhortation and prayer, the mural decorations represented figures and scenes from ancient mythology altered so as to apply to the biblical stories. It is not probable that in music alone a different course was pursued and pagan influence entirely set aside. A strong argument in favour of this view is based on the discovery that most of the hymns and antiphons of the Roman Church conform to the melodic types (nomes) peculiar to the Greek hymns and choral songs accompanied by the kythara, a large lyre, to which on account of the fixed pitch of its seven strings these types were best adapted. The use of instruments at divine service being prohibited, the accompaniment was either omitted or, as some authorities claim, supplied by the voices of the musically better informed members of the congregation.

In the Eastern Church, and through it later in the Western Church, the influence of Hebrew music made itself felt. Philo (20 B.C.–A.D. 40), a Hellenistic Jewish philosopher, wrote of the Therapeutæ, the sect referred to in the previous chapter, that they continued to celebrate their love-feasts in the following manner: After the Supper, when all had risen, two choirs, one of men and one of women, were selected, and from each of these a person of majestic form was chosen to lead. These then chanted hymns in honour of God, composed in different measures and modulations, now singing together and now answering each other by turns. Here the responsive and antiphonal manner of singing which was practised among the Hebrews from time immemorial and was probably introduced into the church by Hebrew converts, is evidently referred to. Another feature for which the Church is indebted to Hebrew tradition, and to which the so-called sequences still in use in the Latin Church owe their origin, were the "pneumæ," florid groups of tones, prolonged shouts of joy, as it were, which were sung by the congregation, at first to the last vowel sound of the word Hallelujah, and later to an inarticulate syllable. It is stated that the Copts, descendants of the ancient Egyptians, who have remained true to the traditions of the Christian Church in Egypt, still embellish their ritual with guttural ornaments and often spin out a Hallelujah to the duration of a quarter of an hour.

It was natural that, as the Christian congre-

gations increased in number and size, efforts
should have been made to render the services
more elaborate for the sake of the worshippers
themselves as well as for the purpose of attracting the public. This led to the introduction of melodies unsuited to church use both
on account of their character and their difficulty; wherefore Clement of Alexandria (died
about A.D. 220) felt called upon to interdict the
use in his congregation of so-called chromatic
melodies, probably melodies which contained
ornaments with chromatic tones.

The popularity which choral music enjoyed
among the Christians is shown by the fact that
in the fourth century the singing of hymns
proved a powerful means in the hands of the
Arians to increase their following. Ephraem
of Edessa (died about 373), the champion of the
Orthodox, and himself a writer of hymns, in
self-defence organised and trained a choir of
young women, with the aid of which he gained
the day. At Constantinople the Arians, who
were not permitted to worship within the walls,
came into the city and congregating at public
places sang antiphonal songs all night long.
Fearful of the result, St. Chrysostom (347?–
407) organised with the assistance and at the
expense of Eudoxia, the Empress of Arcadius,
nightly processional hymn singing, in which

the church singers under their conductor, the
Empress's chief eunuch, took part to the dis-
comfiture of the Arians. From this it appears
that trained choirs belonged to the established
institutions of the Greek Church as early as the
fourth century.

In the Latin Church, which with Rome as
its head was destined to direct the course of
church music, the first step towards bringing order into the chaos of conflicting traditions was
taken with the foundation of singing-schools
at Rome by Pope Sylvester in 314. This was
one of the most noteworthy occurrences in the
history of choral culture, for it led to the organisation of the oldest choral body in the
world, the Sistine Chapel, nominally at least
still in existence, which served as the prototype for all choral institutions up to the time
when, about the end of the eighteenth century,
amateur singing societies, independent of all
church affiliations, sprang into life.

The monopoly of church music — the only
music recognised as artistic up to the sixteenth
century, when secular music began to engage
the serious attention of composers,—was given
to the trained choirs by the decree passed at
the Council of Laodicea in 367, which forbad
all except those appointed therefor to sing in
church. The object of this step was not so

much to encourage choral culture as to bring
uniformity into the music of the ritual and,
after this had been accomplished, to insure
its faithful preservation by tradition; for with
the closing of the pagan schools by order
of Emperor Theodosius (346–395), what little
knowledge of the Greek system of notation by
means of uncial letters had been preserved fell
into oblivion among the people.

To memorise so large a number of hymns and
chants as were in constant use required distinctively musical talent, and to sing them properly,
long technical training. In consequence the
singing schools of themselves developed into institutions for the general musical as well as the
specifically vocal instruction of men and boys of
exceptional gifts. The more proficient these
became, the more forcefully they felt and the
more gladly they yielded to the seductive power
of music for stimulating individual fancy and
breaking the shackles of conventionality and
tradition; and thus there arose the conflict between the progressive efforts of the singers
and the restraining hand of the ecclesiastical
authorities, which continued throughout the
whole course of evolution of church music.

The first effective measures towards adjusting
and prescribing the music of the liturgy were
taken by St. Ambrose, Bishop of Milan (340?–

397), who sifted the material which had accumulated in the course of time and enriched the Roman ritual by bringing antiphonal and responsive singing as well as Greek hymnody from the Eastern to the Western Church. He also translated a number of the most beautiful Greek hymns into Latin and wrote new ones in the latter language. These hymns were of simple rhythmical structure, principally in the iambic metres peculiar to Greek popular poetry, and were probably intended to be sung to melodies of a Greek type, for St. Augustine (354–430), the collaborator of St. Ambrose, is credited with having made a collection of such melodies for church use. The oft repeated story that St. Ambrose excluded all melodies excepting those which conformed to four certain Greek modes or scale forms, afterwards called authentic, has been long since disproved.

The influence of the singing schools became more and more apparent in the course of time. The ecclesiastics, who were trained in these institutions from boyhood up and began their activity as members of the choir, became so interested in their musical studies that they neglected their other duties. It was their one aim to excel in beauty of tone production, smoothness of execution, and expressiveness of utterance. They could not be restrained from

27

altering the prescribed melodies by unduly pro-
longing tones, spinning out traditional tone-
groups (pneumæ), and introducing new embellishments. There was imminent danger of the
secularisation of church music, of the church's
being turned into a concert room.

To remedy this state of affairs Pope Gregory
the Great (540?–604) induced the synod of 595
to pass among other corrective measures a decree which prohibited priests and deacons from
assuming the specifically musical functions of
divine service and assigned these to ecclesiastics of inferior ranks. Furthermore, he was instrumental in bringing about the reorganisa-
tion of the singing schools which led directly
to the permanent establishment of the Sistine
Chapel. Of the many other musical and liturgical reforms which are persistently attributed
to Gregory the Great, he was not the origi-
nator. Least of all was he responsible for the
introduction of the so-called plagal modes and
of the system of musical notation by means of
the first seven letters of the Latin alphabet.
These innovations belong to a later date, as
does the so-called Gregorian antiphonary,
which was in all probability the work of Gregory II. (Pope 715–731) or of Gregory III. (Pope
731–741). Yet tradition would have it that
Gregory the Great compiled this book of

hymns, chants, and melodies, and caused a copy of it to be made and chained to the altar of St. Peter's at Rome, as containing the only readings authorised by the Church.

The view that there was an essential difference between Ambrosian and Gregorian music is no longer universally entertained. If one was more measured and stately than the other it was the music of the Ambrosian hymn, which was intended for popular, congregational use, not that of the Gregorian chant, which was intrusted to trained choirs. The latter was not deprived of its original embellishments and rhythmic life, nor written in notes of equal value, as *cantus planus*, plain chant, until the mediæval composers made use of it for the purpose of building up contrapuntal riddles.

The Gregorian antiphonary was written in neumes, characters consisting of points, lines, accents, hooks, curves, and angles, which, placed over the syllables of the words of the text, indicated by their contours the directions in which the voice was to modulate. They were probably invented by the singers themselves, who found the Greek system of notation by means of letters (whether Greek or Latin), if they were familiar with it, too intricate. The neumes were nothing more than mnemonic guides with the aid of which only melodies previously learned could be recalled. For the notation of unknown melodies they were useless, as they indicated the direction but not the distance which the voice should cover in ascending or descending. Yet such assistance as they afforded was invaluable, for in the course of the Church year no fewer than one thousand different melodies were sung, some of them only once annually.

The purpose of notation in neumes was identical with that underlying the modern system of notation, which is intended to suggest to the eye the outlines of melody. Some of the conventional embellishments in use to-day, such as certain forms of the trill and the turn, are expressed in signs traceable to the neumes, while the notation of Gregorian music still employed really consists in neumes placed on a stave of four lines. The plan of making these signs more definite by means of a horizontal line seems to have been devised in the tenth century. The object of this line, a red one, was to designate F as the basic tone, so to speak, about which the tone groups represented by the neumes hovered. Therewith one of the principles of the stave notation was practically discovered.

The following example in early neume notation will make apparent the inadequacy and intricacy of the system :—

SOLUTION.

Besides the knowledge of the meaning of the neumes, of which there were as many as forty or fifty, thorough familiarity with the traditions of the Gregorian song was indispensable to its correct performance. These traditions were in constant danger of being distorted and were indeed eventually lost. Even the care which was exercised in the singing schools, and particularly in the Papal choir, the Sistine Chapel, which was the court of last resort in controversies pertaining to the Latin liturgy, was not sufficient to preserve traditions inviolate. The nature of these traditions can be gathered from one of the oldest antiphonaries in existence, that preserved in the library of the convent at St. Gall, Switzerland. This supposedly faithful transcript of the Gregorian antiphonary was supplied, probably by a certain Romanus, who brought it to St. Gall about 790, with the initial letters of words designative of the proper rhythms, variations in speed, ornaments, and vocal effects. Among the last named mediæval annotators mention the tremolo, which they liken to the pealing of the trumpet; the *trillo caprino* ("goat-bleat"), and the *gruppetti*, which are compared to the tendrils of the vine — proof conclusive that the Gregorian chant as originally sung was not plain.

In order to commit to memory such readings and to master the technical difficulties which they presented, long continued study and constant practice were necessary. For both the monastic schools, which were everywhere founded as the most efficient means of spreading the new doctrine, provided ample opportunity. They were modelled after the singing schools of Rome, *scholæ cantorum*, whose curriculum was as follows: One hour was devoted to the study of intonation; a second, to the practice of trills and ornaments; a third, to the practice of scales; a fourth, to acquiring beauty and taste of expression. From time to time the choristers were taken just outsied the Porta Angelica, where, on account of a perfect echo, they could hear their own voices and judge of the effect of their singing. To this course of technical preparation there must be added instruction in reading the hieroglyphic neumes and the rehearsals necessary to all but memorise an endless number of chants and responses. Singers so trained from youth up could not but attain to a high degree of proficiency, and it is not difficult to understand that Gregorian music, homophone though it was, performed by a choir of such singers, in perfect accord with the ceremonial, should not only have produced a deep impression but satisfied the highest artistic requirements as well.

Progress in choral music was not possible in Italy, where the slightest deviation from the rules and traditions observed by the Roman singers was considered a sacrilege punishable with imprisonment. Not so in the erstwhile barbarian countries of middle and northern Europe, where, notwithstanding unremitting efforts to introduce and preserve the authentic Gregorian style with the help of choristers summoned from Rome, national idiosyncrasies could not be suppressed nor the influence of primeval customs effaced. To such an idiosyncrasy the origin of the sequences, a kind

33

of hymn which enjoyed great popularity in mediæval times, is ascribed.

It is said that the Gallic singers with their coarse, ponderous voices were unable to execute the pneumæ with any degree of rapidity and that, in consequence, these florid tone groups were so prolonged as to lose their character and meaning. To prevent their complete corruption they were provided with texts, termed proses because their rhythms depended upon the accent and not, as was the case in classic poetry, on the quantity of the syllables. The most important result of writing sequences (so called on account of their following the verses and antiphons in the ritual) lay in the reversal of the heretofore observed principle that melody should have no identity of its own, but should be the slave of the words, whereas in the sequences the words were adjusted to a given melody, and therewith the independence of melody was practically illustrated. Notker Balbulus (840–912), of the monastery of St. Gall, famed far and wide for the excellence of its boys' choir, was one of the most celebrated authors of sequences. Of the many which were incorporated into mediæval office books in the course of time only five are now recognised by the Church. The two best known of these are the "Stabat Mater," generally attrib-

uted to Jacobus de Benedictis (died 1306), and
the "Dies Iræ," ascribed to Thomas of Celano
(died about 1255).

To the tenacity with which the peoples of
Northern Europe adhered to their old customs
in the face of the opposition of the Church, the
invention of harmony too is in all probability
due. While in Italy the exclusion of instrumental music from the Church was rigidly
enforced, such was not the case in England,
France, and Germany, to use modern geo-
graphical designations. Here under stress of
popular demand the clergy not only permitted,
but encouraged the playing of instruments by
providing opportunities for their study in the
monastic schools. The choir of the monastery
of St. Gall, celebrated for the elaborateness of
its musical services, was on festival days supported by an orchestra of harps (*nablia*), flutes,
an organ, cymbals, a seven stringed psaltery,
triangle, and bells; while the band of the abbey
of Reichenau, an island in the Lake of Con-
stance, was noted for its completeness and
excellence.

Among the stringed instruments in common
use in the northern countries there were several
which were designed to produce a number of
different tones simultaneously; and in imitat-
ing these instruments the choir singers are

supposed to have stumbled on a sort of harmony. On the other hand the fact that those singers versed in the science of adding a new part, the "organum," to a given melody were called organisers, gives colour to the view that the roughly constructed organs in use at the time, the clumsy keys of which were pressed down with the fists or elbows and the tones of which were likened unto thunder, may have been occasionally so manipulated as to sound tones simultaneously, and thus may have suggested the new style of singing.

At first the parts extemporised by the organisers were nothing more than the melody duplicated at the distance of the perfect octave, fourth, and fifth—the only intervals at which it could be accurately reproduced within a certain compass without the introduction of sharps or flats, then virtually unknown. As it is well nigh inconceivable that a continuous series of fourths and fifths should not have offended the musical sensibilities, the theory has been advanced that the different voices did not sing together but followed one another, and in very slow time, thus "breaking" and thereby softening the objectionable intervals. In support of this argument the explicit instructions to this effect given in a treatise on music by Elias Salamonis (about 1274), a monk of the convent of

St. Astère, Périgord, are quoted. Mozart, however, in a letter written during his Italian tour
of 1769 and 1770 refers with surprise to a practice apparently then still prevalent of singing
the same melody at the uniform distance of a
fifth.

Once suggested, the possibility of singing in
several parts stimulated choristers to all kinds
of experiments, which resulted in the invention
of different types of the organum. To one
singer it occurred that he might sustain a lower
tone as a basis to his companion's melody;
another found that he could sustain a tone for a
time and then accompany his associate at the
distance of a fourth or fifth; while a third one,
still more venturesome, dared to proceed occasionally with his voice in a direction contrary
to that taken by his companion who followed
the course of a familiar tune. Thus step by
step the resources of singing in several parts
were discovered.

All this was accomplished in the study room
of the choir. Composers in the real sense of
the word there were none. Until a method of
notation capable of designating the duration of
tones as well as their pitch came into common use, music in two or more parts was
the product of the momentary inspiration of
the choristers; and as the leading ones at least

were required to possess this faculty as well as intimate familiarity with the restrictions to be observed in its exercise, it is evident that the choirs of that period must have consisted of highly endowed, thoroughly instructed, and well trained singers and musicians. The organisers were, so to speak, the soloists of the choirs and were specially paid for their services.

While the organum was developing in practice in the singing schools, theorists were occupied with formulating laws which might apply to the new style. The first treatise on the subject is generally ascribed to Hucbald (840–930), a Benedictine monk of the convent of St. Amand sur l'Elnon, in Flanders (though his identity is not definitely established), and the name of Hucbald is therefore commonly associated with the origin of the organum. Notwithstanding the apparently harmonic character of the organum, neither the singers nor the theorists of that period had a conception of harmony in the present meaning of the term. They had learned to follow the course of two or more melodies independently of each other, but the effect produced by a number of simultaneously sounding tones (chords) they could not comprehend.

Although Hucbald also thought out several new systems of musical notation, his inventions

in this direction proved of no permanent value.
It remained for Guido of Arezzo (born about
995), a Benedictine monk, to discover the
method of stave notation which in principle is
still in use, and to originate a plan of reading
music at first sight which has its adherents at
the present day. So far as the former is concerned, Guido's innovation consisted in drawing between the two coloured lines employed
before his time to represent the tones F and C,
a black one to stand for A, and in turning to
account both the lines and the spaces for the
purpose of placing the neumes, whereby they
were invested with definite meaning as to pitch.
The second of his inventions, though not so
important, is here considered a little more
closely, because on it are based systems of
reading music which, adapted to the requirements of modern tonality, are still in great
vogue with chorus singers, especially in England and America. The principal ones of these
are the so-called " Fixed Do," " Movable Do,"
and the "Tonic Sol-Fa" systems. It may be
well to premise that Guido alone did not for-
mulate the method about to be described, but
that other theorists contributed their share
towards its development.

Guido's life-object was avowedly to be of
service to the Church by devising means for

lightening the burden of "the little ones," as he called his pupils, and promoting their musical knowledge. The first expedient to which he resorted with this in view was based on the association of ideas, and consisted in impressing on the minds of the pupils a typical melody by comparison with which a new one could readily be learned and fixed in the memory. For this purpose Guido chose a then universally familiar hymn, dating probably from the eighth century, one of a number of different versions of which is as follows :—

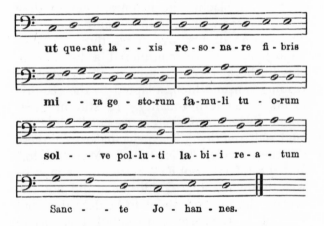

As will be observed, the melody of each of the first six lines of this hymn begins one tone higher than the one preceding. Of this Guido took advantage by teaching his pupils to mentally associate the first syllable of each line with its corresponding tone, without intending however that these syllables should supplant the Latin letters then in common use. His course of reasoning was that whoever succeeded by practice in impressing thoroughly on his mind the beginning of these six verses so as to be able to intone any one at will, would be able to sing any one of the six tones at the mention of its corresponding syllable. Out of this beginning there grew the art of solmisation, which was really based on a principle known to and practically applied by the ancient Greeks—the principle of identifying the interrelation of tones by means of groups of syllables associated with typical groups of tones. In the Greek system the series of fifteen tones which made up the vocal gamut was subdivided into groups of four tones called tetrachords, each of the tones being a whole step or tone distant from the other, excepting the first and second, which were separated by a half step or semitone only (approximately speaking). Each tone of such a group had its name, which, regardless of the actual pitch, made its relation to the other tones of the group apparent. In view of the nature of the ecclesiastical modes Guido subdivided the series of twenty-one tones in use in his time into groups of six tones, hexachords, in which the semitone occurred between the third and fourth tones. For these groups he utilised the syllables above mentioned: *Ut, Re, Mi, Fa, Sol, La.*

Notwithstanding the obvious advantages of the hexachord system, its practical application, especially to melodies of greater range than six tones, required the observance of so many intricate rules—the rules of mutation—that the art of solmisation, as it was called, was by no means an easy one to master. Nevertheless it proved such a boon to the choristers of that period, who were wont to cudgel their brains with deciphering the neumes, as to gain for Guido the fame of being one of the greatest musical benefactors of all times. So glowing were the accounts of the virtues of the new method which reached the Pope, John XIX. (1024–1033), that he summoned Guido to Rome in order to convince himself of their truth. Guido's explanation proved so interesting and lucid that the Pope did not rise from his seat until he had succeeded in singing a verse at first sight.

As the ecclesiastical modes necessitated the change from the Greek tetrachord to the Guidonian hexachord, so modern tonality required the substitution of the group of seven tones, the heptachord, for that of six. This was accomplished towards the end of the sixteenth century, and *Si*, formed from the initials of "Sancte Ioannes," the text of the last line of the hymn quoted, was chosen for the seventh syllable. In the seventeenth century, probably at the suggestion of B. Donati (1593–1647), a celebrated writer on music, *Ut* was supplanted by *Do*, the syllable now universally in use in Italy, England, and America.

A large number of different methods were constructed on the basis of solmisation in the course of time, new sets of syllables with new rules of application being proposed. Of all these methods only the three named now remain in extensive use. The practical value of the syllabic systems of reading music is still under discussion. Only within the last few years a number of leading musicians in England united in urging the abolishment of the Tonic Sol-Fa method, originated by Miss Glover (1785–1867) and perfected by the Rev. Mr. Curwen (1816–1880), which is so popular in that country, and therewith reopened a controversy of long standing. In the schools of America a modified movable Do system still holds its ground in the face of considerable opposition.

III

In the Mediæval Church

WHILE the organisers did not restrict themselves to the use of only those intervals sanctioned by theorists under a misapprehension of the musical system of the Greeks, they were slow to venture on extemporising melodies rhythmically different from the given one for fear of creating confusion among the singers. Nevertheless the seductive charm of creative activity led to experiments in this direction too, and thus in the course of time the art of discant originated. Its home was France, the country in which the sense of harmony appears to have developed most rapidly up to a certain point.

There were two kinds of discant, the simple and the florid. The latter of these signalised the most decided improvement on the organum, for its rules permitted the introduction of ornaments, so-called *fleurettes*, which involved the adjustment of entire groups of tones to a single tone of the given melody and demonstrated the availability of intervals formerly

prohibited in theory. Discant was at first practised in two parts only, to the lower of which,
the tenor ("the holder"), the task of carrying
or holding the *cantus firmus* was intrusted,
while the upper one took charge of inventing
the discant, the counter-melody. In the course
of time additional parts, called *motetus, triplum*
and *quadruplum*, were added—terms which were
not intended to designate particular varieties
of voices but simply to indicate the order of
the parts, the tenor being the lowest. To triplum, the "third" part, treble, the English designation for the highest voice in the chorus is
traced. Its German equivalent *diskant* comes
from discant. The term soprano, the "highest" is of later origin. For motetus, the ety-
mology of which is obscure, the designations
medius and *altus*, the "middle" and "high"
parts respectively, were subsequently adopted,
as was *bassus*, "base," for the lowest part.

It is evident that to invent on the spur of the
moment more or less florid companion melodies
required, besides natural aptitude, a degree of
judgment which could be attained only by long
study and experience. This accounts for the
fact that the practice of discant was intrusted
to men only and was limited for a time to two
or at most three parts. When, however, as
was to be expected, certain melodic turns and

the methods of applying them became conventional, boys could be taught to fit in simple
parts, and discanting in four and more voices
became practicable.

The impulse which the art of discant gave to
choral culture in France was extraordinary.
The singing schools of France had ever since
their establishment in the sixth century enjoyed
the reputation of being among the best in Chris-
tendom.   In promoting the knowledge of discanting they became superior to all others.
Not only were the institutions already in existence provided with the best instructors of the
new style, but schools, *maîtrises*, were founded
for the special purpose of teaching it to the
young, and the royal chapel, organised by Pepin
in 752, was turned at the command of Philip
IV. (1285–1304) into a body of model discanters.
The practice of discanting actually became a
mania.   The members of the choruses and chapels who were particularly proficient in this art
were in great demand, and the standing of a
body of singers was decided by the number and
excellence of the discanters of which it could
boast.   As with constant practice the singers
acquired the ability to extemporise with more
freedom, they took pride in embellishing their
part more and more richly, so that, in addition
to inventiveness and judgment, technical skill

46

in vocalisation became indispensable to their equipment.

In their efforts to outdo their colleagues some discanters conceived the idea of singing two or even three given, generally well known melodies at the same time, making such changes only as were necessary to avoid too disagreeable consequences. Confusion became worse confounded when other voices attempted to add something new to such combinations. The melodies chosen for elaboration were not only Gregorian chants but folk-melodies as well, the original words of which were retained without any thought and certainly without any intention of offending piety. This practice, which was not discontinued until towards the end of the sixteenth century, was, notwithstanding its objectionable features, of benefit to music, because it helped to counteract the prevailing mechanical, calculative tendency by the introduction of the vitalising power of the French folk-song.

So long as two or even as many as four singers accustomed to each other's methods and idiosyncrasies joined in discanting, serious misunderstandings could be avoided, but when a whole chorus attempted to do so, disastrous results were inevitable. This hastened the invention and perfection of a system of notation by means of which the relative duration of tones could be designated. It was the outcome of a series of practical experiments made one by one by the discanters, not the discovery of a single mind. Music written according to this system was called measured music, *musica mensurata*, in contradistinction to plain music, *musica plana*, the unisonous Gregorian chant, in which the duration of tones was originally determined by the prosodical rules governing the Latin text. The chorale notes in which the Gregorian chant is written to this day, although identical in shape with the measured notes, do not stand for definite relative values. They are nothing more than simplified neumes.

One of the first treatises on measured music was compiled either by a Franco of Cologne, who lived during the latter part of the eleventh century, or by one of several Francos who are believed to have flourished a century or more later. The characters in use about that period were neumes which had been transformed for practical reasons into notes with black square, oblong, and lozenge-shaped heads. Each of these notes represented twice the value of one of the next lower denomination until the church composers adopted the ratio of three to one also, as symbolical of the Holy Trinity, and for a time (during the twelfth and thirteenth centuries) wrote almost exclusively in triple metre. The complications to which this subdivision of the same symbols into different relative values gave rise, were increased by an intricate system of metrical signatures and rules which made of measured music a mathematical science and placed almost insurmountable difficulties in the way of the choristers who were compelled to decipher them. Yet the general principle upon which measured music rested furnished the basis for modern musical notation.

Measured music did not introduce the element of rhythmic organisation into the tone-art. The measured notes were simply technical devices calculated to facilitate singing in parts. For rhythmic design, by which is meant the symmetrical arrangement of tone groups of clearly comprehensible rhythmic structure, music is not indebted to the works of the church composers, even the greatest among them, but to the folk-song and the instrumental dance-forms cultivated by the people.

In the hundred and fifty years, from about 1150 to 1300, during which measured music was practised side by side and in connection with discant, such progress was made in the formulation of rules for writing in a number of parts that the close of the period of tentative effort began to dawn and musical composition began to enter the sphere of art,—the art of counterpoint. This differed from written discant and was superior to it in that the parts added to one or two given melodies were not tones or tone groups strung together at random, but melodies as organic and coherent as the ones with which they were to be associated. As, notwithstanding the apparent individuality of each melody, every tone in its relation to the other simultaneously sounding tones was subject to the severe rules of polyphony then considered binding, pieces so constructed were said to be in counterpoint, point against point, or note against note.

Neither political nor artistic conditions in France were favourable to the full development of the new style of music which had originated there. It fell to the lot of the Netherlands to bring the technics of counterpoint to perfection in the course of the two hundred years following. From the middle of the fourteenth to the middle of the sixteenth century the Flemish masters held almost exclusive sway over the musical destinies of Europe.

Although with counterpoint composition in the real sense of the word was introduced and a limit was set to the extemporaneous efforts of the choristers, progress in music continued to rest largely with these, for with but few exceptions the great church composers were members of celebrated choirs and gained their knowledge and experience in choristers' schools. Nor was the art of discant neglected as the practice of carefully writing out all the parts of a choral composition obtained vogue. The *cantus supra librum* or *contrapunto a mente*, as mental counterpoint was called in contradistinction to written counterpoint, afforded a rich field to singers for the exercise of their talents in discanting. Mental counterpoint, extemporising in the contrapuntal style, was practised in the churches of Italy up to the present century, choristers versed in it being much sought and more liberally remunerated than those who could sing by note only. Improvising was considered the supreme test of musicianship. On his Italian tour of 1770, Mozart, then a lad of fourteen, was frequently requested to submit to this ordeal and was acclaimed a genius on the strength of the ease with which he passed it; and sixty years later Mendelssohn challenged universal admiration by the occasional display of his gift of improvisation. That Bach required his pupils to play on the spur of the moment accompaniments in the contrapuntal manner is well known.

Difficult as it was to master the intricacies of reading measured notation under any circum-

stances, it was made doubly so by the aberrations into which composers were led in their
efforts to arrive at the highest possible degree
of excellence in the technics of composition.
To decipher the contrapuntal riddles which
the choristers were expected to solve almost
offhand was a task worthy of the efforts of the
best educated musician. These riddles were
not originally thought out for their own sake
or in order to puzzle the singer, but for the
purpose of enabling the composer to keep intact, to the eye at least, the contours of the
prescribed short Gregorian chant or of the
folk-song on which an entire mass or a long
motet (an elaborate form of polyphonic composition on freely chosen sacred words) was
based. As the constant repetition by the tenor
of the same melody would have unavoidably
become monotonous, the composer formed
new melodies without changing the notation
of the original one by requiring the singers to
resort to such devices as reading the notes
backward; reversing the direction of the intervals without altering the intervals themselves; lengthening or shortening one or more
tones; or introducing occasional rests. The
rules for the guidance of the singers, which
were generally given in metaphorical mottoes
often couched in obscure Latin verse, were

called canons, whence the designation canon, now applied to a composition constructed strictly according to the rules of imitation.

Quite as difficult to figure out were the intricacies which composers delighted in creating on the basis of the subtle metrical system of measured music. It became customary to change the metre frequently in the course of a piece, not uniformly in all the parts, but in each part independent of the others, so that it was often necessary to sing simultaneously groups, which, consisting of such combinations as those of four, five, eight and twelve tones, clashed metrically. These were indicated not by the simple methods now employed but by means of signatures with the application of which to the notes, which remained unaltered in shape, the singer was expected to be perfectly familiar. The climax of artifice, however, was reached when composers wrote masses or motets for four or more parts on one stave, the notes on which each of the parts was compelled to read in a different metre and even in frequently changing metres. In the following example the opening measures of such a riddle, a "fugue for four parts out of a single one" by Pierre de la Rue (born about 1450), are given in their original form and in their solution. On examination it will be found that the same melody is assigned to all the four parts in as many different metres.

Fuga quatuor vocum ex unica (Petrus Platensis).

SOLUTION.

The introduction of the more elaborate forms of discant and counterpoint made necessary the organisation of select choirs of adults who devoted themselves to the practice of the florid style, while the ordinary choirs of boys and men confined their efforts to the Gregorian chants harmonised in a rhythmically uniform manner. Being dependent on the select choirs for the performance of their works, composers were, therefore, limited to the comparatively small compass of male voices. Efforts to find a way out of this serious difficulty suggested

54

the expedient of singing in falsetto, which by
the fifteenth century resulted in the extension
of the vocal scale to three octaves, whereas in
the eleventh century it had covered little more
than two octaves, reaching up to about B
(on the third line of the stave with the G or
treble clef). The male alto or counter-tenor,
generally a baritone or bass trained in the use
of the falsetto, is still to be found in the cathedral choirs and glee clubs of England. In the
sixteenth century the range admissible in
choral music was practically exhausted by the
discovery in Spain of a secret which enabled
male singers to command the whole compass
of the boy or woman soprano. These Spanish
singers were in great demand until they were
in part displaced in the course of the seventeenth century by the artificial male sopranos,
who eventually became the tyrants of the Italian operatic stage. In the church choirs of
Italy and Southern Germany such singers were
preferably employed as principals, though not
to the exclusion of boys and natural falsettos,
up to the nineteenth century. In 1745, when
Haydn was a member of the choir of St.
Stephen's, Vienna, there were about a dozen
artificial male sopranos in the Austrian Imperial chapel. In Italy they are not unknown at
the present day. In France and England, how-

ever, their sphere of activity was confined to the Italian opera, boy sopranos being preferred for choirs.

The mediæval composers divided the voices at their disposal into two classes : the acute, embracing boys' voices and the voices of the natural and artificial adult male sopranos and altos; and the grave, embracing men's voices in their normal state. The parts for the former they called cantus and altus, those for the latter tenor and bassus. In employing the different higher or lower varieties of these classes with a view towards producing the desired tone effects they displayed the greatest skill, and for the purpose of clearly designating these varieties made use of an elaborate system of clefs. The classification of voices now current is, of course, of recent date and gradually crystallised under the influence of the Italian opera singers and composers.

No less influential than the Flemish composers were the Flemish choristers. It was largely owing to the superiority of the latter that church choirs assumed the dignity of artistic institutions and were converted from bodies of clericals instructed by monks in the tradition of the Church, into organisations of professional singers and musicians trained by the best masters and ambitious of promotion

and fame. The Flemish singers were celebrated all over Europe. In Italy, France, and
Germany it was a cause for constant complaint
that these foreign choristers were in greater
demand and more liberally remunerated than
the native ones. It was the highest ambition
of kings and princes to have in their chapels as
many Netherlanders as possible and, above all,
to be able to boast of a Netherland chapel master, for whom no honours and emoluments were
considered too great.

The history of the chapel of Duke Albert of
Munich, of which Orlando di Lasso (1532–1594),
the only Flemish master to be compared with
Palestrina, was conductor, may serve to illustrate how some of the celebrated choirs of that
time were organised and trained. Through
the influence of the fabulously wealthy house
of the Fuggers, Lasso was induced to leave
Antwerp and take up his residence in Munich.
He was empowered to bring with him his best
singers and to secure additional ones, as well
as the most competent instrumentalists, wherever they could be found in all Europe. The
boys were domiciled in his own house, towards
the purchase of which the Duke had contributed
a large sum. Here they were under the personal supervision of Lasso, who instructed them
in the art of singing and in the theory of music,

not, however, to the neglect of their general
education. Appreciative of the advantages of
studying under so great a master, many of the
boys returned after their voices had changed,
so that in the course of time the chapel consisted of boys and men who, with but few
exceptions, had been trained from the very
beginning by Lasso himself. This choir remained under his direction for thirty-seven
years. The chapel in its entirety embraced
twelve basses, fifteen tenors, thirteen adult male
altos, sixteen boy sopranos, five or six artificial
male sopranos (*musici*), and thirty instrumentalists. With such resources at his command
Lasso, who according to all accounts was not
only a severe disciplinarian but an inspiring
conductor as well, must have attained results
of the surpassing excellence of which it is difficult to form an adequate conception. The
singing of the choir is said to have been supremely beautiful in quality and perfectly balanced, and not to have been marred by the
slightest deviation from the pitch even in the
longest unaccompanied composition. At banquets it was customary for the orchestra to play
until dessert had been served, when the choir
under the personal direction of Lasso performed a programme consisting of choruses,
and quartets and trios given by picked voices.

Such establishments, however, were not often to be found outside royal courts, wherefore they were called *scholæ palatinæ*, Imperial singing schools, while the most highly developed polyphonic style of singing, to which such bodies only were perfectly equal, was called the *mos palatinus*, the Imperial style up to the seventeenth century.

As was inevitable, a reaction against artificiality in composition set in after the possibilities of contrapuntal technics had been fully exploited by the Flemish masters, and when the power of sensuous beauty inherent in harmony began to assert itself. Towards this the growing cultivation of secular music largely contributed. Although in secular music too the polyphonic style was the prevailing one, folk-songs naturally suggested a less severe treatment than the mass. Especially was this the case with the shorter forms, such as the "Frottole," street songs, the "Cacce," hunting songs, the "Ballate," dance songs, and the "Falas," bright, rapid movements sung to unmeaning syllables. The most highly organised type of secular music was the madrigal—usually interpreted to signify a shepherd's song—to which the church composers devoted particular attention, and which was subsequently transferred to the early operas.

The singing of madrigals and contrapuntal arrangements of popular songs was extensively practised in private circles and was encouraged, even participated in, by the nobility. Andreas Pevernage (1543–1591), master of singing in the Cathedral of Antwerp, arranged weekly choral performances in his home for the purpose of familiarising his friends with the newest works in choral literature. In Paris Baif, the founder of the Academy of Poetry and Music, gave weekly choral entertainments in which Charles IX. (King of France 1560–1584), who was a well trained tenor singer, participated. In Italy chorus singing was fostered at the courts of the nobility, such as the Sforza at Mantua, the Este at Milan, and the Medici at Florence; and in Rome Leo X. (Pope 1513–1521) supported at great expense a number of celebrated virtuosi to entertain him with playing and singing secular music.

While the Flemish composers made disciples among the Italians as early as the middle of the fifteenth century, it was not until a hundred years later that the master appeared who turned the eyes of the musical world from the Netherlands to Italy. That master was Palestrina (1526–1594), and the type of music which he created was not an Italian one, but the highest and purest type of unaccompanied polyphonic ecclesiastical music of all countries and of all times.

The technical superiority of Palestrina's music lies in this—that while each and every melody of the polyphonic structure is vocally fluent and individually expressive, and is of equal significance with every other melody, the harmonies which result from the union of all the melodies are so supremely beautiful and succeed each other so naturally as to preclude the thought of calculation. It is the apparent artlessness of the tone combinations, which are really the product of the most profound learning, that is so eloquent of his consummate skill, for the simplest harmonic progressions often prove on close examination to rest on the most intricate forms of imitation.

Of much greater importance, however, than the technical are the spiritual qualities of his music. Palestrina's conception of what the music of the Roman Church should be was in perfect accord with the principle held by the Early Church: that music should form an integral part of the liturgy and add to its impressiveness. This had been lost sight of in the effort to develop the mechanics of composition. Palestrina by force of his sovereign command of all possible resources created a type which, notwithstanding its high artistic organisation, never obtrudes its own beauty, but reflects, or perhaps it might be better to say refracts, in its exalted and chaste purity the ineffable mysteries symbolised in the ceremonies of the Church. For its full effect, therefore, his music is dependent on its association with the ceremonies, the spiritual contemplation of which had inspired it to the smallest detail. No sensuous melodies, no dissonant, tension-creating harmonies, no abrupt rhythms distract the thoughts and excite the sensibilities. Chains of consonant chords growing out of the combination of smoothly flowing, closely interwoven parts, the contours of which are all but lost in the maze of tones, lull the mind into that state of submission to indefinite impressions which makes it susceptible to the mystic influence of the ceremonial and turns it away from worldly things.

Such melodies and harmonies as Palestrina wrote and such effects as he produced by different groupings of the voices were possible only under the system of ecclesiastical modes; to the modern system of tonality they are foreign. Progress on the lines followed by Palestrina was impossible. With him the golden era of vocal counterpoint came to an end. Even during his lifetime the opponents of polyphony, the champions of the dramatic style, began to assert themselves, and instrumental music to encroach on the domain of vocal music.

Up to 1305 the papal chapel at Rome, or singing guild, as it was then called, had been the means of preserving the Gregorian musical ritual as accurately as was possible by tradition. In that year, however, a new choir was formed at Avignon, whither the pontifical court had been transferred. Under Benedict (Pope 1334–1342) such emoluments, generally in the shape of ecclesiastical preferments to which special indulgences were annexed, were assured the members of this choir that the services of the most celebrated singers and composers of France and the Netherlands could be secured. In consequence the chapel, now numbering twelve, became an organisation of virtuosi and musicians whose pride lay in the introduction of the most advanced methods. This new choir was part of the brilliant retinue with which Gregory re-entered Rome on January 17, 1377. Under the name of pontifical chapel it supplanted the old singing school and, liberally endowed by Eugene IV. (Pope 1431–1447), developed into a cosmopolitan university for church music, in which foreign artists predominated until Roman composers and singers had mastered the polyphonic style. The number of its members was increased from twelve to twenty-four, and finally to thirty-two, the figure which has represented its normal strength since 1625. About the year 1441 the places of the boy choristers were taken by adult falsetto singers, largely Spaniards. The first artificial soprano was admitted into the choir in 1601. This class of voices has been represented in the papal chapel ever since, subject to certain conditions. The Sistine Chapel, famous for the frescoes by Michael Angelo, was added to the Vatican in 1473 by Pope Sixtus IV., and as it was here that the papal choir daily officiated, the choir itself became known by that name. In the same year Sixtus IV. erected a choral chapel in St. Peter's which he provided with a body of choristers who were subject to the jurisdiction of the papal singers. This choir, consisting of from fifteen to twenty boys and men, which was called the Julian Chapel after it had been liberally endowed by Pope Julius II. (1503–1513), has remained to the present day the official choral body of the Basilica of St. Peter. Its singing is often taken by the uninformed for that of the Sistine Chapel. The latter was practically disbanded when on September 20, 1870, the Sardinian troops entered Rome and the temporal power of the Pope came to an end, although its members are gathered together on special occasions to sing in the Sistine Chapel. Don Lorenzo Perosi, the young composer in whom the devotees of Italian church music are placing their hopes, was appointed honorary master of the papal chapel in 1898. It is said that he is making efforts to obtain permission to introduce women's voices into the choir. While the singing of the Sistine Chapel has always been unaccompanied, the Julian Chapel has the support of two organs, and two groups of double basses and 'cellos, placed opposite each other with the two sections into which the choir is divided for the purpose of producing antiphonal effects.

The Sistine Chapel, with which the activity of Palestrina as a composer was so long identified, has remained the authority for the proper performance of his music. The traditions essential thereto concern not only unimportant details but radical features of the Palestrina style. They affect even the very tones themselves, for on account of theoretical punctilios chromatic signs were very sparingly used in writing, singers being expected to introduce them in accordance with the rules of *musica ficta*, artificial music. This was strikingly illustrated when the choristers of the Imperial chapel at Vienna attempted to sing the celebrated Miserere by Allegri (1584–1662), which Mozart as a lad of fourteen wrote out from memory after having heard it twice. As a special favour a faithful copy of this Miserere, which was guarded with jealous care by the Sistine Chapel, was sent to Emperor Leopold (1640–1705); yet the effect of its performance by the Imperial choir was so disappointing, owing to the unfamiliarity of the singers with the correct reading of the text, the traditional ornaments, and the proper manner of shading the music, that the papal chapel master was unjustly accused of having forwarded a garbled version. Besides introducing the *abellimenti*, as the unwritten ornaments are called, the Sistine choristers constantly varied the tempo and produced peculiar tonal effects by means of imperceptibly increasing and decreasing the number of voices in accord with certain acts of the celebrant at the altar, all of which was necessary to the realisation of the composer's purpose. As by far the greater number of the compositions in the repertory of the Sistine Chapel were written by the members themselves, the application of the methods in vogue with that body of singers was a foregone conclusion. Unless performed accordingly, such compositions must, therefore, fail of fully expressing the authors' intentions.

IV

After the Reformation

WHEN in 597 St. Augustine accompanied by a number of Roman choristers came to the county of Kent to introduce Gregorian song into England, his teachings and the instruction of his associates were so eagerly received and intelligently followed that in a short time English singers became famous the whole Continent over. Since then choral culture in England has not suffered any interruption save that which took place from 1649 to 1660 under the Commonwealth. Not only were the monastic and cathedral schools, modelled after those of Rome, of the best, and the endowments for ecclesiastical and lay choristers ample, but secular institutions too for the propagation of musical learning were encouraged by the clergy. In 849 a chair of music was created in the Oxford High School, though in all probability for the study of music as a science only, and as early as 1463 the University of Cambridge conferred the degrees of bachelor and doctor of

music. Gerald de Berry (1146–1220), Bishop of
St. David's, said of the Welsh and the inhabitants of the north of England that they did not
sing in unison like the inhabitants of other
countries but in as many parts as there were
singers, who all "finally unite in consonance
and organic melody under the softness of B flat."
On the borders of Yorkshire he found that the
people sang in two parts only, a habit which
was so deeply rooted that the children adopted
it as soon as they began to sing. Foreigners
who visited England during the fifteenth century declared the chorus singing in that country to be equal to any to be heard on the Continent, and asserted that in the cultivation of
secular music the English were in advance of
all other peoples. During the reign of Elizabeth (1558–1603) the city of London advertised
the musical abilities of the boys educated in
Bridewell and Christ's Hospital as a means of
commending them as servants, apprentices, or
husbandmen. Even while the organum and
discant were in a rudimentary state in France
there was practised in England the more ma-
ture method of harmonising melodies known as
the Fa-burden (*fauxbourdon*), which consisted
in accompanying each tone of a given melody
with its third and sixth, whereby an unbroken
series of consonant chords was formed ; and

evidences are accumulating that the art of counterpoint too originated in England, and that
Dunstable (died 1453), a native of Dunstable in
Berfordshire, was one of its earliest exponents.
Then for a time English composers yielded
precedence to their Flemish contemporaries,
and while they achieved admirable results in
the current forms of the mass, motet, and madrigal, it remained for the Reformation to in-
spire them with the energy necessary to the
establishment of an English national school of
music.

Although since the days of Wycliffe (died
1384) psalms were chanted in English, it was
not until about the middle of the sixteenth
century, when Marbeck's Book of Common
Prayer appeared, that the musical possibilities
inherent in the English cathedral service began to be duly appreciated and the unlimited
field of activity to be exploited which presented
itself in the harmonisation, and in the adaptation
of plain song melodies to English words, in the
composition of hymns to the metrical transcrip-
tions of the psalms, and in the setting of the
canticles in the form of anthems.

For the hymns English composers did not
have such resources to fall back upon as
Luther and his collaborators had found in the
German folk-melodies. Hymn texts, therefore,

seem for a time to have been composed somewhat elaborately after the manner of short
motets. Soon, however, such settings gave
way to the popular tunes in use among the
Protestants at Geneva. These together with
others of the same character, traceable partly
to German and partly to English sources, furnished the nucleus of early English hymnody.
The first collection of hymn tunes for four
voices, harmonised in the plainest manner with
the melody in the tenor, appeared in 1563. In
a collection published in 1591 the melody was
given to the highest part, probably for the first
time. The most celebrated volume of hymns,
however, was the one edited by Ravenscroft and issued in 1621. Not only are the
tunes of this collection truly devotional, but
their arrangements in plain counterpoint, with
the melody in the tenor, are models of good
taste and in their very simplicity disclose perfect command of the technics of polyphonic
writing. That such melodies and such settings
should have been cast aside for the inferior,
unchurchly ones which obtained vogue after
the Restoration and are in common use to-day,
is to be deeply deplored.

A distinctively English form of church music, and the form in which the achievements of
the English polyphonists culminated, was that

of the anthem. This took the place of the Latin
motet when the Latin language was banished
from the Church in England. The full (choral)
anthems of such masters as Tallis (died 1585),
Byrd (1538–1623), and Gibbons (1583–1625), are
among the choicest specimens of unaccompanied contrapuntal composition. The accompanied (verse) anthem for soloists and chorus
belongs to the period of decadence of the pure
church style, which was hastened by the
French tastes of Charles II. (1660–1685). The
permission to embody the anthem in the liturgy, granted by Queen Elizabeth in 1559,
is notable for its accompanying injunction :—
" having respect that the sentence of the hymn
may be understanded and perceived,"—a quali-
fication which anticipated by four years the
similar demand made by the commission of
Pope Pius IV. for the reformation of church
music and satisfied with such important results
by Palestrina.

Secular music of an artistic standard was
represented in England principally by the madrigal, which stood in high favour with the nobility and gentry, and to which the English polyphonists imparted a national character. At
the time of Henry VIII. (1509–1547), who was
himself a composer of high attainments, it was
considered a disgrace not to be able to carry a

part in singing a madrigal. When, however, counterpoint succumbed to modern harmony the madrigal made way for the less elaborate glee, and for the round and the catch, peculiarly English types of music the correct performance of which became a difficult art with fixed traditions, properly understood only in England to this day. Singing catches with appropriate gestures, as was customary, formed one of the principal amusements at the court of Charles II., and was enthusiastically taken up by the common people particularly of the northern and midland counties, where aptitude and love for part-singing were present to an unusual degree.

In the Chapel Royal England possesses one of the oldest, if not the oldest, choral institutions in existence with the exception of the Sistine Chapel in Rome. Although the first record of such an establishment dates back to the fifteenth century only, it scarcely admits of doubt that royal chapels were organised long before that time. From that record it appears that the Chapel Royal of Edward IV. (1441–1483) was complete in every department and was conducted on an elaborate scale. It consisted of a Confessor to the Household; twenty-four Chaplains and Clerks, skilled in discant, eloquence in reading, and ability in organ play-

ing; two Epistlers, ex-chorister boys; eight
Children and a Master of the Children. The
members of the chapel were bound to accompany the sovereign wherever he might go.
The children were boarded and lodged at the
royal palace. They had daily amongst them
"two loaves, one messe of greate meate, ij
galones of ale," and were attended by one servant "to traine and bear their harness and
lyvery in Courte." When on a journey with
the king's chapel they received fourpence a
day for horse hire. When their voices changed
"yf they will assente the King assygneth them
to a College of Oxford or Cambridge of his
foundation, there to be at fynding and studye
both suffytyently, tylle the King may other-
wise advance them."

While in the Chapel Royal and at St. Paul's
in London the children were evidently well
cared for, such seems not to have been the case
at churches of minor importance. Officers were
constantly roaming the country with warrants
empowering them to seize and take with them
for service in the royal chapel singing men
and children "with good breasts" and expert
in the science of music, wherever they could
be found, whether in cathedrals, churches,
colleges, chapels, houses of religion, or any
other place within the realm. The right of

carrying out this edict seems to have been surreptitiously exercised in favour of other choirs
than those for whose benefit it had been framed,
and the boys so impressed appear not always
to have been well treated, as the following complaint written by Thomas Tusser (1523–1580),
the author of " Five Hundred Points of Good
Husbandry," when he was chorister at Walling-
ford, indicates:—

> " Oh shameful time! for every crime
>   What toosed ears, like baited beares.
>   What bobbed lippes, what yerkes, what nips,
>   What hellish toies!
>   What robes, how bare, what colledge fare,
>   What bread, how stale ; what penny ale,
>   Then Wallingford, how wert thou abhor'd
>   Of silly boies."

The life of the choristers, however, was not
altogether one of discipline and work. They
enjoyed from the earliest times certain privileges and rights from the exercise of which
they derived a little money and a great deal of
amusement. They were permitted, for instance, during a number of days every year,
generally in December, to impersonate their
superiors and assume authority over them.
In doing this they displayed such skill in acting that they were intrusted with the performance of miracle plays and, at the time of

74

Queen Elizabeth, even with the representation of masques and dramatic pieces. Under Edward VI. (1547–1553) the royal chapel, consisting of thirty-four singers and thirty-nine instrumentalists, was maintained at an annual expense of more than twenty - two hundred pounds sterling.

The singing of the royal choristers must have been on a high plane of excellence. A Venetian ambassador at the court of King Henry VIII., who had undoubtedly often heard the services at St. Mark's in Venice, which the great Flemish master Willaert (1480–1562) had made famous, wrote "the mass was sung by His Majesty's choristers, whose voices are more heavenly than human. They did no chant like men, but gave praise like angels."

Fortunately the reign of the bigoted Roundheads, who in waging a war of extermination on everything associated with the conduct of the ritual of the Anglican Church directed their efforts towards the complete extinction of choral culture, not excepting the singing of catches and glees in ale-houses, was not of sufficient duration to quite destroy musical traditions. Nevertheless, when under Charles II. cathedral music was restored, so much difficulty was experienced in obtaining choir-boys that it was frequently found necessary to supply their places in the chorus with adult falsetto singers and even cornets. For the Chapel Royal, however, Captain Cooke, once a chorister of the chapel of Charles I., succeeded in gathering together a set of boys of most extraordinary talent. On one occasion the King, who took great pride in his choir, after having appealed in vain to his court composers to finish at a few hours' notice a thanksgiving anthem for the celebration of a victory over the Dutch fleet, communicated his wish to these young choristers. Undaunted three of them undertook and accomplished the task within the allotted time by writing the piece known as the "Club Anthem." These three boys, Humphrey (1647–1674), Blow (1648–1708), and Turner (1651–1739), grew up to take their places among the most celebrated composers of that period, and together with their fellow chorister, Henry Purcell (1658–1695), one of the greatest if not the greatest of English-born musicians of all times, became the founders of the new English school of church music.

Naturally in sympathy with the dramatic movement following the Renaissance, which bore music from the ecclesiastical modes and the unaccompanied polyphonic style towards modern tonality and the accompanied monodic style, these choristers were urged on in

Henricus Purcell.

the new direction by Charles II., who, having acquired a decided taste for the melodious and brilliant French operatic music during his stay on the Continent, insisted on its introduction into the Church. Accordingly he commanded his composers to write bright, tuneful pieces in which the solo voices would be duly considered and interludes frequently introduced for the orchestra of viols, sackbuts (trombones), and cornets with which he filled the organ loft of the royal chapel. In complying with his wishes they created the verse anthem with its short melodious and more or less florid movements for solo voices, chorus, and organ or orchestra. Purcell's works in this form as well as in the larger choral forms, such as those of the sacred cantata and the ode, were of so advanced a type and showed so keen an appreciation of the means of characteristic expression inherent in musíc that Handel felt safe in accepting them as models for his early compositions of the same kind. Influences similar to those which dictated the substitution of the verse for the full anthem, were responsible for the supplanting of the time honoured unisonous Gregorian with the modern harmonised single and double chant.

With the introduction of Christianity into Germany provisions were made for the instruc-

tion of the clergy and choir-boys in the proper
performance of the Roman ritual by the foundation of schools in Fulda in 744 and shortly after in Ratisbon, Würzburg, Mayence, and other
cities, similar to the Roman singing schools and
presided over or inspected at intervals by Roman choristers. The people being necessarily
debarred from participation in the regular services of the church, which were conducted in
Latin, sought and found opportunities to give
praise in their own language and in their own
songs at church festivals for which definite liturgical forms had not been provided and which
in the course of time had assumed the character of popular celebrations. In this they were
encouraged by the clergy, who translated Latin
church hymns into the vernacular and wrote
new ones adapted to folk-melodies. Some of
the sequences of Notker Balbulus, already referred to, originated in this way. The folk-
melodies themselves underwent changes in the
course of time under the influence of the Gregorian chants, which the people, who heard
them constantly, involuntarily imitated. This
is particularly observable in many of the tunes
which were introduced in the miracle plays,
the forerunners of the oratorio.

As early as the thirteenth century every
church festival had its *canticum vulgare*, its pop-

ular song, in which the congregation joined either at a designated place in the course of the service or at the end of it. In Bohemia, a country noted for its wealth of beautiful and characteristic folk-music, the singing of spiritual songs was made the subject of special study. With this purpose in view the first choral society of which there is any record was organised at Prague in 1195. This was the "Society of Chorus Singers," and its expressed object was the improvement of popular sacred music. Its mission was later taken up by the "Choruses of Literati," singing societies established by students of seminaries and universities in order to promote congregational singing in the vernacular. In Germany similar movements were begun towards the end of the fourteenth century.

Notwithstanding the fact that interest in sacred music was widespread in Germany, the practice of discant and counterpoint yielded no important results in that country until the Reformation necessitated the introduction of a new type of church composition by revolutionising the liturgy. Up to that time the German polyphonic composers followed in the footsteps of the Flemish masters; and while some of them, such as Finck (about 1500) and Isaak (died about 1517), the composer of the noble tune "Inspruck ich muss dich lassen," which Bach so often made use of, applied the Flemish methods with conspicuous success to German folk-melodies and spiritual songs, they did not found a distinctively national school.

All this was changed by the Reformation. The individual, personal nature of the new doctrine not only permitted but required the employment of the vernacular and the participation of the congregation in divine service. In order to encourage this Luther (1483–1546) advocated the retention of the most familiar hymns of the Latin Church, which he translated into German, and the introduction of popular folk-songs and spiritual songs, the texts of which he and his collaborators adapted for church use. This was the origin of the Protestant chorale. In the course of time new tunes were added, Luther himself being a contributor. The melody of the Battle Hymn of the Reformation, " Ein' feste Burg," however, generally ascribed to him, was composed by Walther (1496–1570). Luther, who loved music and had studied it in the schools of Mansfeld, Magdeburg, and Eisenach, insisted that these melodies should be harmonised artistically—which meant in the polyphonic manner then prevalent—yet so as not to distort or make unrecognisable their contours. Rupf, chapel-master to the Elector of Saxony, and Johann Walther, cantor at the court of Frederick the Wise at Torgau, accomplished this task. The first collection of chorales collated and edited by Walther was published in 1524 at Wittenberg in five books, each containing a single vocal part only. In this collection the melody with but a few exceptions was given to the tenor, while in later hymn-books the principle of assigning the leading part to the highest voice, so successfully carried out in the arrangements for congregational use made by Dr. Lucas Oseander and published in 1586, was almost universally adopted. One of the most characteristic features of the chorales, particularly of those resting on folk-tunes, was the irregularity of their metrical construction, the combination of duple and triple metre. This peculiarity was unfortunately sacrificed in the course of time to the efforts of the organists to extemporise elaborate polyphonic accompaniments. The German chorale in tones of uniform value, as now sung, is but a shadow of its original self.

Great importance though Luther attached to congregational singing, he did not fail to advocate the retention of trained choirs and thereby to encourage the composition of choral music in the more elaborate forms. In writing such works the German composers remained true to the dignified style becoming the church, and to

this it was due that polyphonic methods were
not entirely forgotten when the monodists of
Italy and France became the musical lawgivers.

In the perpetuation and improvement of the
schools for the education of choristers, which
had been founded under the Roman Church,
Luther took an active interest. Having himself received his musical instruction in monastic and cathedral schools and realising the
need of such institutions, he appealed to civic
authorities, parishes, and wealthy citizens to aid
in supporting them when, with the secularisation of bishoprics and with the suppression of
abbeys and the alienation of their lands, they
and the choirs connected with them were dissolved. Luther had been a " poor scholar " too
and one of the *currendani,* who earned a spare
penny by singing hymns and spiritual songs
before the houses of the well-to-do; and having
learned from observation the religious influence of this practice, he urged its continuance.
In addition he advocated the formation of societies for the propagation of church music.

While on the one hand church choirs necessarily sacrificed some of their efficiency for a
time with the loss of the compact organisation
due to their semi-clerical character, they on
the other hand became the means of diffusing
musical knowledge among the people as they

ceased to be hedged in by monastic regula-
tions. Among the institutions which helped
to usher in the new era in choral culture that
of the *currendi* was one of the most efficient.
Although justification for its existence had long
since passed, such an institution was stubbornly
kept alive in Berlin for the pecuniary return
it yielded until about twenty years ago, when
it was prohibited from continuing its practices.

The idea of organising peregrinating choirs
for the purpose of disseminating religious doc-
trines among the people and at the same time
of providing means for the indigent scholars, is
generally ascribed to Scipio Damianus, Bishop
of Asti (died 1472), yet from time immemorial
it was one of the privileges of the pupils of the
monastic schools on certain festival days to
go about town with appropriate emblems and
invite the bestowal of alms by singing. In
the course of the Reformation these juvenile
choirs, the currendi, not only served as a po-
tent means of spreading the new doctrine, but
became an important feature as well in the propagation of choral culture. The currendani, as
the members of the currendi were called, were
selected from the lower classes of the parochial
and cathedral schools and instructed to assist at
divine service by singing choral responses and
chorales. As many of them were poor boys,

and the remuneration for these duties, if there was any, was trifling, they were encouraged to pass from house to house and sing canticles in two or three parts, for which they received a small compensation. In the course of time it became customary to engage their services on every possible opportunity, for in Germany no ceremony or celebration was considered complete without its musical accompaniment. At baptisms, on birthdays, at weddings, and on countless similar occasions the currendani were in demand, so that they were often about from early in the morning till late at night. Whatever the little singers received was handed to the teacher, who at the end of the week divided it up and, after having given to each one the amount necessary for his sustenance, held what remained in trust until the end of the school-term. Daily instruction in singing and in the music of the ritual was given gratuitously. The celebrated English historian Burney, who was much amused at the little choristers, describes them as wearing " black undertaker-like uniforms and large grizzle wigs," and asserts that in the larger cities they received a thaler every quarter of a year from the resident ambassadors for agreeing *not* to sing before their doors. In order to avoid conflict the currendani were divided into a number of choirs

to each of which a certain territory was assigned.

In the higher, the Latin schools, especially
in those connected with cathedrals, the custom of making provisions for the lodging and
boarding of a number of boys and youths within the school enclosures, generally old monas-
teries, remained in force after the Reformation.
In return for the enjoyment of these privileges
the alumni, as these boys were called, were
bound to serve as members of the church choir
or of the church orchestra, when instrumental
accompaniment was required, for they received
not only vocal but instrumental instruction as
well.   The funds requisite for the sustenance of
additional alumni were often furnished by persons interested in church music.   In some parishes as many as fifty alumni were provided
for.

On these choirs devolved the duty of singing
the figurate music, music written in florid counterpoint, to which the little currendani were
not equal, and to them belongs the credit of
having popularised in Germany the works of
the polyphonic masters, which had been until
then cultivated almost exclusively by the royal
and princely chapels, composed largely of
Flemish and Italian singers.

The alumni were really competent musicians,

many of whom looked forward to a professional career. The only drawback to the efficiency of the choruses of alumni was that the tenors and basses lacked the sonority of maturity, while the sopranos and altos could serve for a short time only, on account of approaching change of voice. It is said that it was not unusual for a lad of seventeen to sing a soprano solo of a Sunday and a few weeks later to be one of the basses.

A phenomenon for which it is difficult to account is that the secret which made it possible for male adults to sing high soprano parts, and which was supposed to be known to the Spaniards alone, appears to have been in the possession of some of these young men. Spitta, the biographer of Bach, whose testimony is unimpeachable, asserts that it was not uncommon for the adult choristers who sang the solos in Bach's works to command a range up to E and F in Alt., and Burney writing in 1732 from Vienna referred in laudatory terms to the singing in falsetto of the "poor pupils." In Dresden the chorus for the Grand Opera even was made up of the alumni of the School of the Holy Cross from 1717 till 1817, when Carl Maria von Weber organised a special opera chorus.

As the alumni, like the currendani, were permitted to sing in private houses and in this way derived considerable income, applicants for admission into such choirs were numerous, and conductors could, therefore, be exacting in their demands. Bach himself at the age of fifteen left Ohrdruf for Lüneburg in order to apply for such a position, which, of course, he obtained. That the alumni were technically well trained is evident from the requirements which the works of Bach and his contemporaries, composed with such singers in view, make on skill in intonation and execution. The ability to surmount easily such difficulties as those of rapid scales and trills was considered absolutely indispensable to the equipment of a chorister.

The influence of the currendani and alumni on choral culture in Germany was highly beneficial. Even after their official connection with church choirs had ceased, the former boy choristers as students at the seminaries and universities continued to manifest their interest in choral music by establishing choruses and participating in the services of the church. Together with the *adjuvantes*, voluntary assistants, who reinforced the instrumentalists regularly employed, they made it possible to undertake the elaborate production of large accompanied choral works, especially on festival days. At the University of Leipsic, for instance, a *chorus musicus* was organised in the sixteenth century for the purpose of adding interest to the aca-

demic functions by means of musical performances. This chorus, the members of which
were former alumni, was endowed by the government and became so celebrated in the course
of time that churches were glad to obtain their
cantors (directors) from its ranks.

The students also formed *collegia musica*, institutions the origin of which is attributed to
Jodocus Willichus (born 1501), who is said to
have organised the first society of this kind at
the university of Frankfort-on-the-Oder. The
members of these societies generally met in
taverns, where they played and sang for their
own pleasure as well as for that of a few invited friends and then enjoyed a repast.
The collegium musicum founded by Telemann
(1681–1767), a prominent composer and influential musician, gave performances in the New
Church which attracted wide-spread attention,
especially during the Leipsic Fair, on account
of their brilliant operatic style, to the disadvan-
tage of the dignified services in the Church of
St. Thomas conducted by Bach, who eventually superseded Telemann. To such societies
institutions like the Gewandhaus Orchestra of
Leipsic are to be traced.

In the smaller towns, where the means for
supporting alumni were not at hand the music
lovers, many of whom had been currendani in

their youth, constituted themselves into choirs
and made it possible to sing figurate music in
co-operation with the boy choirs. They furnished instrumental accompaniment too on
church festivals. These *cantoreyen*, as they were
called after their instructors and directors, the
cantors (originally *rectores chori*), were the suc-
cessors of the religious brotherhoods which
were common in Switzerland and Bohemia in
the twelfth century and had Cecilia for their
patron saint.

One of the oldest and most long lived of
such cantoreyen, and a typical one, was that at
Torgau, which supplanted the chapel of the
Elector of Saxony, Frederick the Wise (1544–
1556), and was founded by Walther, a member
of that chapel and afterwards Luther's adviser.
This cantorey organised from among the towns-
people "for the elevation of public divine service by artistic singing, if possible with the
accompaniment of instrumental music," became a guild which enjoyed the protection of
the town council and the assistance of the
wealthy citizens. It was the pride of the whole
community and its services were in frequent
demand. In the course of time it was turned
into a society resembling in many respects the
singing clubs of to-day. In 1596 associate
members, as they would now be called, were

admitted. The entrance fee for these was a goodly quantity of Torgau beer. Once a year a *convivium musicum*, a banquet with music, was arranged, towards the expense of which each member contributed his share. In these celebrations the chorister boys were allowed to join, "it is to be hoped by partaking of the edibles only" adds the serious minded chronicler. For being late at rehearsals the active members were fined five pfennige, about a cent and a half, for each quarter of an hour. Absence from a rehearsal was punished with a fine of three groschen, about six cents. The cantor was authorised to summon the singers for practice whenever he considered it necessary. In 1628, it was resolved that "pleasing music" should be performed at the annual banquet, which Otto Taubert (1811–1891), the chronicler referred to, and himself cantor at Torgau for a time, declares to have been the first effort at cultivating secular music among the middle classes. Simultaneously with this innovation the initiation fee was fixed at fifteen thalers for passive, and five thalers for active members, from the payment of which, however, the clergy, town waits (musicians authorised by law to follow their calling), and organists were exempt. The chorus at that time numbered twenty-five, and the limit of membership for the whole society was set at sixty. This association was wrecked, as were most of its kind, by the gradual preponderance of its social over its musical interests. Its musical activity ceased in 1735, but its annual banquets took place until 1771. The cantoreyen were the forerunners of the modern amateur choral and orchestral societies.

With the decline of religious enthusiasm and the decadence of musical taste due to the growing popularity of the Italian operatic style, the institutions which had fostered the highest types of polyphonic choral music passed away. The choruses of currendani, of alumni, and of students at seminaries and universities, with isolated exceptions, died out for want of moral and material support. But the love of music which they had sown in the hearts of the German people of every class and which in the course of time made the German nation the most musical of all nations, never grew cold. Choral culture only lay dormant for a time, to be reawakened to new and more beautiful life than ever with the organisation of amateur choral societies.

V

The Mystery. Bach

"THE Passion," by which is meant the gospel narrative of Christ's Passion set to music wholly or in part, is the most elaborate representative of a type of dramatico-ecclesiastical functions the origin of which can be traced to remote antiquity. The original designation "mystery" as a collective title for such functions, the retention of which Spitta has suggested, is to be advocated because it keeps before the mind their source, character, and purpose, and serves to facilitate the differentiation between the Passion and the oratorio proper, which is essential to the correct understanding of both.

The prototypes of the Christian mysteries are to be found in the Egyptian mysteries of Osiris, the Indian mysteries of Vishnu, the Greek mysteries of Dionysus, and the Roman mysteries of Bacchus, all of which were religious festivals instituted to commemorate and propitiate the deities at certain periods of the year.

The Mystery

Just as with the Greeks a high art form, the drama, grew out of the Dionysiac mysteries, so one of the highest types of choral music, the oratorio, ultimately developed out of the popular Christian mysteries, without, however, displacing the original ecclesiastical functions themselves in which they were rooted and which the strong hand of the Church restored again and again to their sacred dignity and has preserved in their pristine purity to the present day.

The early Christian hymnographers, especially those of the Eastern Church, followed classic models both as to their metrical forms and their dramatic construction not only as a matter of taste but as a matter of policy as well. The last Olympic games took place in 394, while in Rome pantomimes with choral and orchestral music, representing incidents from heathen mythology were not suppressed, notwithstanding Imperial decrees, until a century later, and it was largely for the purpose of furnishing a substitute for such performances that the hymn-writers frequently cast their compositions for the celebration of church festivals into a form not unlike that of the Greek drama.

One of the oldest known plays, or rather mysteries, of this kind is attributed to Gregory of Nazianzen, patriarch of Constantinople from 380 to 381. It treated the history of the Passion in the shape of a dialogue interspersed with hymns corresponding to the choruses of the dramas of Æschylus and Sophocles.

Of the cycles of hymns of Romanus and his followers written in the course of the sixth and seventh centuries, a number have been preserved. One of these by Romanus himself, intended for Christmas or Epiphany, embraces an account of the Nativity and its wonders; a dialogue between the wise men, the Virgin mother, and Joseph; a scene representing the arrival of the magi, who tell of the religious conditions of Persia and the East, recount the cause and adventures of their journey, and offer their gifts; a scene picturing the Virgin interceding for them with her Son and instructing them in Jewish history; and a closing prayer for the salvation of the world. The style of the hymns of which this is an example, indicates that they were intended to be sung —possibly with instrumental accompaniment. They were used at divine service and collected in hymn books which remained in great favour until the tenth century, when they were no longer recognised as church books. That similarly constructed poems were current in the Western Church admits of no doubt.

The Mystery

With the adoption of the Gregorian antiphonary, which in effect eliminated congregational
singing from the liturgy, the opportunities for
incorporating such hymns into the ritual necessarily disappeared. On the other hand the
possibilities inherent in the liturgical forms for
investing the gospel narrative with something
like dramatic interest by the aid of illustrative
living pictures and vocal music, were taken advantage of by the clergy, especially on festival
days, as early as the fifth century, and the people themselves were encouraged to supplement
the church ceremonies by commemorating the
great events in sacred history in a manner not
unlike that of the traditional pagan celebrations.
In the course of time the church festivals became popular festivals, and such they have remained to the present time. Even in Protestant Germany the principal feast days of the
Church are popular holidays the religious im-
port of which is almost forgotten.

There were two influences at work, then, in
shaping the mysteries: the one coming from
the Church and having for its basis the liturgy; the other coming from the people and
having for its source the dramatic and spectacular performances of the pre-Christian era. Out
of the former, principally, grew the liturgical
mysteries which culminated in Bach's Passions;

out of the latter, the popular mysteries and moralities which became the prototypes for the oratorio and opera.

In order to bring home as forcibly as possible to the understanding of the people the signifi- cance of the leading incidents from sacred his- tory which the church festivals commemorate, the custom became prevalent about the eighth century of giving prominence to the personal elements in the gospel narrative by distributing the chanted dialogue among a number of differ- ent officiating ecclesiastics and assigning the utterances of the various groups, such as those of the shepherds in the Christmas story, the disciples and the people in the Passion and Easter stories, to all of them combined. It is not improbable that occasionally scenic decora- tions were arranged in front of the altar, fitting costumes donned by the clergy, and histrionics moderately resorted to. Further than this no effort was made at dramatisation, nor were the scenic adjuncts really sanctioned by the Church.

At such representations the official language of the Church, Latin, and the authorised melo- dies of the Gregorian chant were used through- out, the impersonators being the priests, their assistants, and the choristers.

This method was perpetuated by the papal singers, by whom the Passion was celebrated in the following manner: The gospel texts were chanted to the prescribed Gregorian tones, without any accompaniment whatever, by three ecclesiastics, called Deacons of the Passion, to one of whom, a bass, were assigned the words of Christ, to another, a tenor, those of the Evangelist, and to the third, an alto, those of the other personages. In the utterances of the people, the *turbæ*, all joined. As the Gregorian melodies suffered changes in the course of their oral transmission, a number of different readings of the chants of the Passion were current in the Sistine Chapel until 1685, when there was published at the command of Pope Sixtus V. the authoritative version which has since been closely followed. About the same time an important innovation was made in the service by the introduction of choral settings of the turbæ. These were provided by Vittoria (1540–1608), one of the most illustrious of Palestrina's followers, who wrote music to the exclamations of the crowd in four parts in the simplest and severest polyphonic style, which was sung by the choristers from the choir in the Sistine Chapel for the first time in 1585 with such effect that the custom has been adhered to ever since. Vittoria's turbæ were not intended to be dramatic in style ; nor would dramatic choruses be in place in association with Gregorian chants and an ecclesiastical function — a fact which Mendelssohn seems to have overlooked when he complained in a letter from Rome to his old teacher Zelter that the turbæ were set to such tame music. Passions of the kind described are termed (Gregorian) chorale Passions.

While Luther recommended the retention by the Protestant Church of the chorale Passion translated into German, he advocated its further artistic development. Accordingly his associate Walther after having written two in the old style in 1552, composed a third one which belongs to a more advanced type in that the choruses, the turbæ, disclose an effort at characteristic expression.

The freer application to the chorale Passion of the newly acquired science of harmony resulted in the motet Passion, in which the whole gospel history, including even the narrative of the Evangelists, was assigned to several solo voices and chorus. Such a one by Gesius (1555?–1613), in which the words of Christ were set for four voices, those of the People for five, those of St. Peter and Pilate for three, and those of the Maid Servant for two, was published in 1588 at Wittenberg. Heinrich Schütz (1585–1672), who transplanted the rapidly maturing methods of the Italian dramatic composers into Germany, applied them unhesitatingly in his "Seven Last Words of Christ," making use of the instrumental resources of the time: an orchestra consisting of a number of keyed instruments and different kinds of lutes and harps. In his Passions, however, probably in deference to tradition, Schütz returned to the purely vocal method, employing the melodic types of the plain chant in the solo passages, but treating them in the new declamatory, recitative like style. The choruses he composed with perfect freedom and imbued with a degree of vigour and descriptiveness which heralded the passing of the chorale and motet Passion and the approach of the dramatic oratorio Passion.

So long as it was considered obligatory to cling to the scriptural text and, in a measure, to the plain chant, there was little opportunity to take advantage of the symmetrically constructed lyrical forms, such as the arioso and the aria with orchestral accompaniment, which the Italian dramatic composers had called into life. The steps necessary to remove this difficulty were boldly taken by Sebastiani, organist and chapel-master at Brandenburg, in 1672. Sebastiani not only interlarded the gospel narrative of his Passion with verses of chorales, the melodies of which he arranged for solo voices in the form of the aria, but also wrote

original recitatives to take the place of the
plain chant and added an orchestral accompaniment for strings (large and small viols of from
five to seven strings each), organ, a " positive "
(small portable organ), harpsichord, lutes, and
theorbe (bass lutes). Therewith the chorale
Passion received its death - blow and the oratorio Passion was created in which free scope
was given to composers for the application of
the means of musical expression in vogue in
the lyric drama.

An attempt to raise all the barriers between
the oratorio and the Passion was made by the
poet Hunold, who in his " Passion Story of
the Bleeding and Dying Christ " treated the
sacred story after the manner of an opera text.
Noteworthy features of this poem were the
soliloquies, emotionally contemplative com-
mentaries on the progress of the action, which
were retained in almost all subsequent Passion
texts and became to Bach, who identified them
with personified poetic ideas, such as "the
Daughter of Zion" and "the Christian Church,"
a medium for the transmission of some of his
most beautiful and tender utterances. Hunold's libretto set to music by Reinhard Keiser
(1674–1739), one of the most prolific opera composers of the Hamburg school, was performed
during Holy Week of 1704.

Reaction against the bold secularisation of the Passion history having set in, efforts were made to remove the most objectionable features at least of such texts. Of the many versions in which this was kept in view, the one by Barthold Heinrich Brockes, a member of the town council of Hamburg, published in 1712, met with the approval of the clergy and at the same time satisfied the requirements of composers. The setting of it which Handel made in 1716 at Hanover was his last composition on a German text. Bach copied the first half of it with his own hand for the purpose of study. The poem by Brockes differed from that by Hunold principally in the reinstatement of the narrator, the Evangelist, and in the reintroduction of the chorale, the elimination of both of which by Hunold had been the principal cause of offence.

At the time of Johann Sebastian Bach (1685–1750) the influence of the Italian dramatists had made serious inroads on church music, particularly on the mystery, the original liturgic character of which had almost entirely been lost sight of. Bach, however, being thoroughly imbued with the true spirit of these church services was enabled by the strength of his genius to restore this spirit and make subservient to it the musical forms and means of expression which had developed under the hands of the Italian composers and toward the elevation of which to the highest artistic dignity he contributed more than any other single master.

So far as the skeleton of the form of Bach's Passions is concerned it does not differ materially from that of the pristine chorale Passion, for it consists of the verbally unaltered Gospel narrative with its dialogues and utterances of the crowd set as of old for single voices and for chorus. About this framework cluster the soliloquies, the reflective passages, which mirror the emotions of the believer as he contemplates the significance of the narrative; and the chorales, the popular (*volksthümliche*) element, which invite the participation of the congregation and threading their way through the entire musical fabric emphasise its Protestant and German character. These diverse constituents Bach not only elaborated with clear judgment and marvellous skill and invested with intense expressive power, but combined into a homogeneous art-work, which, notwithstanding an infinite variety in details, is dominated by the ecclesiastical spirit of the mediæval mystery.

Bach is generally credited with having composed eight mysteries, of which five were Passions, one a Christmas, one an Easter, and one an Ascension mystery. Of his Passions there

BACH.

have been preserved those according to the
Gospels of St. Matthew, St. Luke, St. John, and
fragments of one according to St. Mark. Of
these the Passion according to St. Matthew is
best known by far and is most frequently performed, unfortunately to the all but total neglect of the one according to St. John.

In order fully to grasp the spirit of Bach's
Passions it is necessary to remember that they
were written with their performance as church
services in view. Bach having in mind the ecclesiastical chorale Passion, which was still sung
at his time, particularly in Saxony and Thu-
ringia, studiously avoided introducing extrane-
ous dramatic elements for the sake of effect
merely. The music of Bach's Passions is thoroughly lyric. It is the expression of the religious devotion of his own individual self as
representative of that of his fellow believers.
Even the dramatic portions are not the utterances of actors in a drama, but those of the
Christian congregation which is carried away
in its contemplation of the events to the point of
identifying itself with the actual participants in
the scene. Bach, therefore, did not strive to
individualise the characters concerned in the
Gospel story. The singers who give expression
to the utterances of these personages do not
stand for the characters themselves but speak

for the hearer who passes with them through
the scriptural scenes. One character only did
Bach isolate from all the others and picture in
a distinctly individual color: the character of
the Saviour; and this he accomplished by the
delicate means of the accompaniment, which,
when set to the words of Jesus, is intrusted to the
strings, in contrast to the clavichord, which sup-
ports the other recitatives. It is likewise necessary to the understanding of Bach's Passions to
bear in mind that they are essentially Protestant, services of the people and for the people.
The foundation of their musical structure is the
Protestant chorale, the vernacular of the Protestant Church, as it appears not only in the
simple form suited to the participation of the
congregation, but also in the marvellously beautiful and ingeniously built up choral movements, such as the opening and closing ones of
the first part of the St. Matthew Passion, in
which the chorale is the vital element.

As Bach's Passions are not oratorios, but
spiritual mysteries, in other words, church services, they should be performed amid the sur-
roundings and under the conditions with which
in view they were composed in order to be
thoroughly comprehended and appreciated.
This is all the more necessary as the music of
Bach gains nothing from the adventitious means

of overwhelming volume in chorus or orchestra. Its tissue is so delicate that any attempt to magnify its constituent threads only tends to destroy the exquisite quality of the fabric. Bach's music is as intimate as chamber music. Its strength lies in the noble, elevated, sincere, and heartfelt character of its themes, its beauty, in the perfect harmony between form and content. The subtlety and exhaustiveness with which the prevailing thoughts are elucidated from every point of view cannot be realised without earnest study. Bach's music must be approached in the same loving spirit in which it was written, and with the same patience which was expended on every detail of its construction; for Bach, ever loyal to his Teuton nature and to his reverence for art, gave expression to his innermost emotions in the choicest and most carefully considered manner, unmindful whether his musical language would be easily understood and would appeal directly to his hearers or not, so long as it voiced his own feelings and satisfied his own refined taste and his keenly critical musical sensibilities. Bach's music, therefore, is not for the masses, and it is not strange that even his monumental St. Matthew Passion should have been permitted to lie buried in musical archives for almost a century—until Mendelssohn unearthed it and conducted a performance of it on March 12, 1829, at Berlin.

On the technical resources as well as the artistic perceptivity of the chorus Bach's works make great demands. His was not the ideally vocal style of the mediæval polyphonic composers, who spent their whole lives among choirs only, and to whom choral music was the only artistic music. Bach's younger years were devoted principally to the study of the organ and of organ music, and this determined his style, which tended to the consistent contrapuntal elaboration of themes rather than to the production of specifically choral effects, though he knew well how to achieve these whenever it served his purpose. With the capabilities of his favourite instrument in mind he frequently wrote passages which are more instrumental than vocal in character. To give a transparent and intelligent performance of any of the more difficult works of Bach, not to speak of one which discloses their deeper lying spiritual meaning, is, therefore, not an easy task.

The Passion according to St. Matthew, in its original version, was sung for the first time at the Vesper service of Good Friday, April 15, 1729, at the Church of St. Thomas, Leipsic. In its present revised form it was probably not heard before 1740. It is constructed on a gigantic scale, for two choirs, among which the six soloists are apportioned, two orchestras, and an organ. In the stupendous introductory double chorus a third choir is necessary to carry the chorale which is the key to the movement.

What resources Bach had at hand on that memorable Friday to meet such extraordinary requirements is an interesting question. It can be partially solved with the aid of a letter written by him to the town council of Leipsic shortly after the first performance of the St. Matthew Passion, in which he complained of the inadequacy of his choral and instrumental forces and requested that they be increased. His demands were indeed moderate. He asked for no more than three, or, if possible, four singers (including the soloist) in each part of each of the two church choirs of which he as cantor was the director, and of from eighteen to twenty instrumentalists for each accompanying orchestra. He showed that of the fifty-five alumni in his charge in the school of St. Thomas only seventeen were competent, and that there were only eight musicians who were bound by contract to serve in the orchestra, these eight being three " artist violinists " (professionals), four town pipers, and one apprentice who played the bassoon, " of whose quality and

musical knowledge, however, my modesty for-
bids me to speak," wrote Bach.   In addition to
these he could count on extraordinary occasion for voluntary assistance on the University
choir, of which he was the official musical director, on the amateur students' chorus founded
by Teleman, which Bach likewise conducted at
the time, and on a number of adjuvantes, former
alumni, who continued to take an active interest in church music.   Before his time stipends
had been set aside for the remuneration of
such amateur assistants, but in Bach's day they
were no longer available.

Taking into consideration all these circumstances and the size of the choir gallery of the
Church of St. Thomas, it is safe to say that at
the first performance of the St. Matthew Passion the chorus, including the soloists who, as
was customary, sang with the chorus, stepping
forward when required, numbered from twenty-
four to thirty-two, divided into first and second
chorus, while the orchestra, likewise subdivided,
numbered from forty to forty-five.   Bach conducted, seated at the clavichord, with gestures
and by playing whenever there was any wa-
vering or whenever he considered it necessary
to call attention to dynamic signs.   The chords
in the unaccompanied (*secco*) recitatives were
given by an assistant at the organ.   It is not

known whether the congregation joined in the chorales as it subsequently did and still does at Leipsic with most impressive results. The solos were sung in all probability partly by boys and partly by adult students particularly well trained in the use of the falsetto. These solos were conceived with such interpreters in mind, and therefore, while Bach intended that they should be sung with deep pious devotion, he certainly did not wish them to be imbued with an emotional intensity foreign alike to the music and to the immature natures of those to whom he intrusted them.

The relation between the chorus and orchestra, the latter being more numerous than the former, as was commonly the case in those days, was in perfect accord with Bach's intentions. Bach in his orchestration did not aim for sonority. His music consists of a multitude of individual parts each one of which is of equal importance with every other one, and his instrumentation is therefore calculated to keep intact the individuality of each of these parts rather than to swell the tone volume. For this as well as for the fundamental tone color he relied on the organ, the one instrument which belongs to the church and is closely identified with church music, and the volume of which could readily be accommodated to that of the vocal body. The harmonies for the organ as well as the clavichord accompaniment Bach indicated by means of the figured bass, a kind of musical short-hand employed at that time, which every musician was expected to read and elaborate in good taste. In accordance with the traditions observed in supplying such accompaniments, which were all but lost in the course of time, Robert Franz (1815–1892), as keen a critic as poetic a composer, made complete orchestral scores of "The Passion according to St. Matthew" and of a number of others of Bach's works, adapted to the instruments now in common use. This he did in a spirit of reverence and with a degree of judgment which are above praise.

Not so imposing in dimensions yet no less perfect than the Passions as works of the polyphonic art are Bach's motets and cantatas. While the mediæval masters had invested their motets with a degree of elaborateness second to that of the mass only, the early German composers converted them into simple polyphonic settings of chorales, adapted to the needs of the Protestant Church and to the capabilities of the choirs of the currendani. Bach, however, restored the motet to its old-time dignity of the highest type of unaccompanied church music. The motets of Bach kept his name alive among the more efficient German choirs until it was carried over the whole musical world by the resuscitation of his works in the larger forms.

Unlike the motet, which is as old as counterpoint itself, the cantata was a creation of the monodists and originally was a dramatic composition for one or more solo voices with instrumental accompaniment. Carrisimi (1604–1674) in transplanting it into the church illustrated the possibility of combining contrapuntal workmanship with the new harmonic and melodic methods of the dramatic composers. In Germany the chorale forced its way into the cantata as into every type of Protestant church music. Utilising the various elements of both the dramatic and choral cantata, Bach moulded them into a perfectly balanced and highly organised form. Taking the melodies of appropriate chorales for his principal subject matter, he treated them with all the polyphonic skill at his command and interlarded the choral movements with recitatives, and airs set to metrical texts commentative of the Gospel lessons of the Sundays and festivals of the church year. Bach composed two hundred and ninety-five of such cantatas, which next to the Passions are far and away the loftiest examples of accompanied church music and contain choruses unexcelled even by Bach himself.

In the works of Palestrina the mediæval type of vocal polyphony, which had for its principal object chaste, sensuous beauty, attained the highest perfection; in those of Bach the modern type of polyphony, vocal as well as instrumental, which has for its main purpose the exhaustive exposition of characteristically expressive melodies, reached the fullest development.

VI

The Oratorio. Handel

IN imitation of the semidramatic liturgical ceremonials, and side by side with them, the popular celebrations of the church festivals developed. As has been shown, these substitutes for the pagan religious rites were not only encouraged by the Church but were permitted to take place within the very sacred walls themselves and were even participated in by the clergy. One of the oldest of such popular mysteries, dating possibly from the fifth century, was the *Festum Asinorum* held on the Festival of the Circumcision, when in commemoration of the Flight of the Holy Family into Egypt a richly caparisoned ass bearing on its back a young maiden with a child in her arms was led through the city and finally into the church, followed by a crowd of people who alternately imitated the braying of the animal and sang a carol, the melody of which in a version of the twelfth century has been preserved.

Of a more highly organised type were the miracle plays written by monks for performance by the inmates of the monastic schools. In these the scriptural narrative, the musical setting of which was in the style of the plain chant, was interspersed with explanatory dialogue, while at suitable points folk-melodies provided with fitting words were introduced for the sake of variety as well as in order to give the people opportunities for active participation. The Passion story was utilised for such plays in preference to the Christmas and Easter stories principally because of the superior opportunities it offered for dramatic treatment and spectacular effects, although in Germany the Christmas and Easter celebrations too were popular. In England Passion plays were performed as early as the twelfth century, and there is on record the representation of such a play in 1378 by the choristers of St. Paul with the explicit sanction of the clergy. In 1264 a company of monks was organised in France for the express purpose of performing the " Sufferings of Christ." During the thirteenth and fourteenth centuries it was customary to give miracle plays on a grand scale on every extraordinary occasion. In the Passion play of Oberammergau, which takes place decennially,—the current year (1900) completes such a cycle — this custom has survived by special indulgence.

The scope of the religious plays was enlarged in the course of time by the introduction of subject-matter from the Old Testament and from the legends of the saints of the Church; and, in the "moralities," by the allegorical treatment of religious motives, the characters representing personified virtues or qualities. Of the last mentioned form the troubadours were probably the inventors. Among the most popular subjects were such as "The Good Samaritan," "The Prodigal Son," "The Sacrifice of Abraham," and "The Spiritual Comedy of the Soul." In the same degree as these plays became more highly organised, the musical elements were forced into the background, the use of the plain chant being discontinued and preference given to the spoken dialogue, while the choral movements were reduced to the smallest proportions.

As the miracle plays drifted farther and farther away from the liturgical services in which they had originated, everything that could pander to a taste vitiated by the remnants of the ancient popular entertainments, which were perpetuated in the farces (*farsæ*), was introduced. Devils and the prince of devils became indispensable figures, for to them as the clowns and buffoons of the play the spectators looked for amusement. Even the Passion story was defiled by the addition of vulgarly comic episodes. The costumes were made so elaborate and the scenery so costly that it was impossible for one and the same town to arrange such representations for two successive years. Every link that had bound the popular mysteries to the liturgical mysteries was severed. The Church was compelled to condemn a practice which it had sanctioned for years and which could be purified and chastened only by being elevated to an artistic plane.

About the year 1551 Filippo Neri (1515–1595), a learned priest canonised in 1622, instituted a series of meetings at Rome in the oratory of the monastery San Girolamo, and later in the church of S. Maria in Vallicella, at which he delivered discourses on Scripture history. In order to make these more attractive to his audiences, which consisted of young men of the humbler classes, he prefaced and followed his sermons with narratives of the scenes under consideration cast into the shape of dialogues, which were presented possibly in action, certainly with interspersed spiritual songs (*laudi spirituali*) of the type made popular by the choirs of *laudisti*, organised early in the fourteenth century. Neri's assemblies led to the formation of an educational society of secular priests, which Gregory XIII. sanctioned under the name of *Congregazione dell' Oratorio*. To these circumstances the adoption of the term Oratorio for the religious drama is generally traced, though on somewhat insufficient grounds. No less celebrated a master than Palestrina composed spiritual songs, in madrigal style, for the Congregation of Oratorians.

The development of the oratorio in Rome now went hand in hand with that of the opera in Florence, from which it differed only in the subject-matter. The first effort to apply to the sacred drama the new accompanied melodic style born of the attempt to revive the Greek drama, was made by Emilio del Cavalieri (died 1599), himself one of the originators of declamatory monodic composition. The result of this effort was the oratorio "*La Rappresentazione di Anima e di Corpo*," "Representation of the Soul and the Body," an allegorical piece written by Laura Guidiccioni after the plan of the mediæval mysteries or, more accurately, moralities. The characters in this sacred drama were principally personifications of abstract ideas: the World, Life, Time, Pleasure, the Body, the Soul, the Intellect. The chorus was seated or stood on the stage, and gesticulated while singing. The orchestra embraced one double lyre (a bow-instrument), one clavi-cembalo, one large bass lute (an instrument of the mandolin class), and two flutes. It was placed behind the stage, out of view of the audience, in order that the actors who carried instruments might appear to accompany themselves. The solos were in the declamatory style of that period, the short choruses, of the madrigal type, harmonised in a primitive manner. Detailed instructions for the actors were given. After having described in musical monologues and dialogues the conflict between worldly pleasures and eternal bliss, the characters typical of the former were to symbolise their evanescence by divesting themselves piece by piece of their gaudy ornaments until they appeared as horrible skeletons. If desired, a ballet with choral accompaniment could be executed at the end of the performance. This, the first genuine oratorio, was produced for the first time in February, 1600, at the oratorio of the church founded by Neri, five years after his death and one year after the death of the composer.

Little progress was made in the oratorio until Giacomo Carissimi, of whom mention has been made in connection with the cantata, appeared. This serious minded and admirably equipped composer sharply differentiated be-

tween the opera and oratorio by giving to the
latter an ecclesiastical, not to say liturgical
character. He discouraged spectacular representations as unsuited to the Church by introducing the *historicus*, the narrator, corresponding to the First Deacon of the Passion, and
invested his choruses with breadth and dignity by amalgamating the declamatory with the
polyphonic style.

Notwithstanding the example set by Carissimi, Italian composers were loath to make a
distinction between the opera and the oratorio.
G. A. Bontempi (1624-1705), a composer and
musical thinker of note, did indeed, in the
prefatory remarks to one of his operas, designate the chorus as the determining factor in
the oratorio style, but this principle was not
generally followed in practice, for it required
much less musical knowledge and labour to
write recitatives and arias suited to the display
of technical attainments and therefore calculated to secure the favour of the tyrannical
vocal virtuoso, which was synonymous with
popular success, than to construct contrapuntal
choral movements which could not be sure of
appreciation. Carissimi's illustrious pupil, however, Alessandro Scarlatti (1659–1725), a marvellously prolific composer,—he wrote one hundred and six operas and two hundred masses,

not to speak of oratorios—followed in the footsteps of his teacher. Emulating Carissimi's
polyphonic workmanship and dignity of style
he not only imbued his choral movements with
high artistic qualities but infused life into the
accompaniment of the recitative and cast the
aria into a symmetrical form. The fact that
Handel drew liberally on Carissimi and Scarlatti for the musical subject-matter of his oratorios speaks for the excellence of the work of
these masters.

Material as were the services rendered by
Italian composers to the development of the
principles of modern tonality and rhythm, which
involved definiteness of harmonic design, the
capability of music for characteristic expression had as yet scarcely dawned on their minds.
It remained for George Frederick Handel (1685–
1759), in choral music especially, to apply these
principles to the supreme end of giving utterance to human emotions with all the directness
and force of which that branch of composition
could be made capable. To the accomplish-
ment of this result he brought thorough familiarity with the Italian vocal methods, absolute
mastery of the resources of counterpoint, then
almost forgotten in Italy, and an inexhaustible
fund of plastic melodic types.

Having followed Italian models in his operas

HANDEL.

and in his two Italian oratorios, Handel did
not arrive at the full consciousness of his own
powers and of the direction in which he could
most successfully exert them until he had repeatedly failed in his London operatic ventures
and had learned to realise the fondness of the
English people for sacred choral works. His
first English oratorio, "Esther," he composed as
chapel-master of the Duke of Chandos, a noble-
man of fabulous wealth who lived in regal magnificence in his palace at Cannons, about nine
miles from London, where he maintained a choir
and orchestra. This oratorio was produced for
the first time on August 29, 1720, in the Duke's
beautiful private chapel by his own choristers
and band reinforced with singers and instrumentalists from London, the former from St.
Paul's Cathedral. The Duke, at whose suggestion Handel had undertaken the composition
of "Esther," is said to have given him one
thousand pounds for the work.

With "Esther" Handel renounced his al-
legiance to the Italian opera oratorio and clearly drew the line between the opera and the
oratorio by investing the choruses in the latter
with supreme importance—the final chorus in
"Esther" is remarkable for its length. Yet
this was but a forerunner of his great choral
oratorios, in which the utterances of the in-

dividual characters, however eloquent they may be, must yield precedence to the elemental power and dramatic force with which the chorus presents to the inner eye pictures of soul-life and describes actual occurrences.

Outside the choruses Handel employed the current forms of contemporaneous opera, recitatives and arias of different kinds, though he endowed them with a significance beyond that which they had possessed before. But for a choral style such as his there was no prototype. This was of his own creation and developed under his hands when, taking Purcell's works for his starting-point, he composed on his first visit to London sacred choral music such as the Te Deum for the celebration of the Peace of Utrecht (1713) and the Jubilate, and, during his stay at Cannons, the twelve Chandos anthems, really sacred cantatas.

Notwithstanding his success in these forms Handel allowed twelve years to pass before he again occupied himself seriously with them, and then he did so only under the stress of circumstances.

Handel was at heart a dramatist and remained such a one all his life. His interest was wholly absorbed by the opera, until, having sacrificed a fortune in his operatic ventures and being reduced to the necessity of recouping his losses in some way, he was compelled to turn to the composition of oratorios. This he looked upon at first as a concession to public taste and a departure from dramatic ideals. Ere long, however, he realised that in the direction of the reformation of the oratorio lay his mission and that the fulfilment of this mission did not imply self-suppression, for in the oratorio he was enabled to utilise all the forms of the lyric drama of his time and in addition to take advantage of his matchless powers of choral composition for narrating and depicting dramatic events and enforcing the lessons which they carried with them.

Handel's interest in the oratorio was revived by a peculiar circumstance. On February 27, 1732, Bernhard Gates (1685?–1773), master of the Children of the Chapel Royal, who had assisted at the first performance of " Esther " at Cannons, gave at his house a representation in costume and action of two acts of this oratorio before an invited audience in celebration of Handel's forty-seventh birthday. The chorus, consisting principally of the choristers and gentlemen of the Chapel Royal and Westminster Abbey, was placed after the manner of ancient Greek dramatic performances between the stage and the orchestra, which was composed of members of " Young's Philharmonic

Society" and the "Academy for Ancient Music." The success of this production as well as of two semi-public ones given shortly after was so decided that an unscrupulous speculator proceeded to arrange a public performance of "Esther," which he announced to take place on April 20, 1732. Goaded on by this shameless act of piracy Handel, on April 19th, gave notice of a performance of the same oratorio to take place "By His Majesty's Command" on May 2d, at the King's Theatre in the Haymarket. As, however, Dr. Gibson, then Bishop of London, refused to permit the choristers of the Chapels Royal to sing in costume, even if they held books in their hands, and Handel was dependent on them for giving the work throughout in English, he informed the public in a postscript to the advertisement that there would be no acting on the stage, but that the house would be "fitted up in a decent manner for the audience." So universal was the enthusiasm which this entertainment aroused that Handel was enabled to repeat it five times.

After having made a similar experience with his pastoral "Acis and Galatea," likewise composed at Cannons, Handel could no longer remain in doubt as to the attitude of the English public toward the choral oratorio, even when produced in appropriate scenic environment only, without costumes and action. Nevertheless seven years more elapsed — years heavy with trials and disappointments — before he could persuade himself to devote his energies to the composition and performance of oratorios rather than to operatic undertakings.

This he was finally induced to do by the success attending the series of weekly Lenten oratorio concerts which he began in 1739. These entertainments, which were increased to twice their original number the year following, came to be looked upon as the most brilliant events of the London musical season on account of the superiority of Handel's compositions as well as on account of the excellence of the performances.

So far as it is possible to determine, the chorus on these occasions consisted of almost eighty and the orchestra of about one hundred, to which there were added, as required, the harp, theorbe, clavichord, and organ — most frequently the last two, which at times were doubled. Handel conducted seated at the clavichord or organ.

Although the numbers given indicate a relation between the vocal and instrumental forces the reverse of that now in vogue, there could have been no lack of balance. On the one hand the choir consisted of boys and men who were professional singers and absolutely letter perfect, on the other hand Handel's instrumentation called for the full power of the orchestra only in the climacteric passages, the different instrumental groups being subdivided into principal (*concertante*) and supplementary (*ripieni*) parts, which he could employ at will. The alto part in the chorus was taken by counter-tenors, the compass and quality of whose voices Handel evidently had in view when he wrote such leads as those beginning the well-known choruses in " The Messiah," " And the Glory of the Lord " and " Behold the Lamb of God,"—themes which lose much of their sharpness of outline when sung by female voices. As even at the festivities of the coronation of King George II. at Westminster Abbey in 1727 the choir numbered only forty-seven singers, it is evident that Handel's Lenten performances were conducted on a scale of extraordinary grandeur according to current estimates.

Once convinced that success under existing circumstances lay in the direction of the oratorio, Handel applied himself to composing in this form with the same energy that he had before brought to bear on writing operas. Desirous of retaining the prestige of his concerts he laboured incessantly to have novelties on hand

and brought out every season at least one new oratorio.

Of the twenty-six oratorios and works performed "after the manner of oratorios" which Handel composed, seventeen are on Scriptural subjects, and of these again fourteen are purely dramatic in construction, following the lines of Italian drama, while two : "Israel in Egypt" and "The Messiah," departing from this model, constitute a class of their own. The " Occasional Oratorio" occupies an isolated position. Common to all of these is the prominence given to the chorus ; and herein lies, as already stated, the reformatory character of Handel's activity. It was indispensable to the development of choral music that the polyphonic choral forms, which had remained almost exclusively in the possession of the Church, should be introduced into the concert-room, and this Handel accomplished with his oratorios. For, notwithstanding the fact that they are based on Biblical history, they were composed not with the church but with the concert-room in view, however well they may be adapted to church use when contrasted with the productions of more modern composers.

In preferably selecting his subject - matter from Holy Writ, Handel was undoubtedly guided quite as largely by practical considerations as by religious motives. He had learned from experience that the events in sacred history, with which English audiences were thoroughly familiar, appealed more readily to their understanding and sympathy than those in heathen mythology, with which they were much less conversant. Furthermore, the very character of the choral oratorio invited the choice of subjects which concerned the fates of peoples, of nations, yes, of the whole world; and such subjects of the most heroic type he found in the history of the Hebrew race and (for "The Messiah") in the Gospel story. These he treated in his fourteen purely dramatic oratorios in the conventional Italian manner, always excepting the marvellously expressive, descriptive, and commentative choruses. In "Israel in Egypt" and "The Messiah," however, he departed from this rule and created special forms.

These oratorios too, Handel's greatest and most popular ones, are dramatic in conception notwithstanding their epic form. Although they resemble the liturgical type in that they are built on Scriptural texts only and in that in "Israel in Egypt" the narrator is reinstated, the vividness with which the different scenes are depicted characterises them as being con cert music pure and simple.

It is certainly not unwarranted to assume
that Handel in these two instances chose to
forego the advantages which he might have derived from adopting the scheme of his strictly
dramatic oratorios because of pious reverence.
Neither the manifestations of the power of Je-
hovah, which form the essential subject-matter
of "Israel in Egypt," nor the life and mission
of Christ, of which "The Messiah" treats,
would admit of being cast into dramatic shape
unless it were done after the manner of the
mysteries and in the spirit of an ecclesiastical
function. Handel, whose musical nature was
no longer in sympathy with this type, therefore adopted forms which enabled him to follow his own methods without doing violence
to his feelings and the feelings of every believer.

"Israel in Egypt" grew out of what now
constitutes its second part, "Moses's Song,"
which Handel began four days after the completion of the oratorio "Saul." Realising with
the practised eye of the dramatist that he could
throw "Moses's Song" into relief by the narrative of the incidents which led up to it in
Bible history, he wrote the series of marvellous tone pictures, principally choral, of Israel's
bondage, of the Egyptian plagues, and of Israel's
deliverance, which for depth of pathos, power

of description and suggestion have never been equalled. This stupendous work Handel put on paper in the incredibly short time of twenty-seven days. The indifference with which its first performance, given on April 4, 1739, was received occasioned him deep pain.

Even more comprehensive in scope than "Israel in Egypt" though totally different in character is "The Messiah," in which Handel celebrated the Life of the Saviour, and which comprises the announcement of His Coming, the Passion, the Resurrection, and the Salvation of man. These events are not recounted by a narrator or in dramatic dialogue, but presented in an imaginative, contemplative spirit. Yet the leading scenes pulsate with truly dramatic life, though they are depicted with a degree of reserve which is eloquent of the composer's appreciation of the loftiness of the subject. There is nothing of vague mysticism in the music of "The Messiah," nor does it disclose any attempt at exegetical interpretation of the text. It is eminently human, suffused with reverence yet permeated with the healthy vigour of a strong, impulsive nature which does not hesitate to give bold, even picturesque utterance to its feelings. Any attempt to surround "The Messiah" with the halo of an ecclesiastical function must result, as it only too often does, in robbing the music of much of its expressiveness and force.

The general plan of " The Messiah " originated with Handel. In compiling the text he had the assistance of Charles Jennens, a literary amateur and friend of his, who on account of the princely manner in which he lived was surnamed " Soliman the Magnificent." The composition of " The Messiah " was another of Handel's wonderful achievements, for it occupied him only twenty-four days, from August 22 to September 14, 1741.

The first public performance of "The Messiah" took place under the composer's direction at Dublin on April 13, 1742, in the Music Hall, Fishamble Street, for the benefit of three charities. A public rehearsal, to which all purchasers of tickets for the performance proper, " a most Grand, Polite and Crowded Audience," were admitted was held four days before. On account of the widespread interest excited by this event a request was inserted in the newspapers, that " ladies would be pleased to come without hoops and gentlemen without swords." The seating capacity of the hall was thereby increased from six hundred to seven hundred persons. The success of the work was extraordinary, the consensus of opinion according to *Faulkner's Journal* being that " The Mes-

siah " was " allowed by the greatest judges to
be the finest composition of Musick that was
ever heard."

Handel agreed to give the charities of Dublin the benefit of the first production of this,
his newest oratorio in return for the assistance
rendered him by " The Charitable Musical Society " at a series of concerts of his own music
which he had been invited to conduct by the
Lord Lieutenant of Ireland, and which had
been most liberally patronised. In acknowledgment he was enabled to turn over to the society the sum of four hundred pounds sterling.

The chorus which Handel had at his disposal at this performance numbered about fourteen men and six boys. As to the size of the
orchestra no reliable data seem to be obtainable. Dubourg, an eminent violinist and great
admirer of Handel's, was the leader, and the
State Band, of which he was master, in all probability furnished the nucleus of the instrumentalists, who were augmented by an amateur
orchestra to which members of the highest
nobility belonged. All these forces had been
brought to a high state of efficiency by Handel himself, who was a severe disciplinarian, in
the course of the five months preceding the
performance. In a letter to Jennens he spoke
in enthusiastic terms of both chorus and or-

chestra. The soloists were Signora Avolio, Mrs. Cibber, who afterward became famous for her singing of "He was Despised," Messrs Church and Ralph Rosingrave—all artists admirably equipped for their several tasks.

In London "The Messiah" was not heard until March 23, 1743. It was on this occasion that at the words "For the Lord God omnipotent reigneth" in the "Hallelujah" chorus King George II. arose, and with him the entire audience, and remained standing to the end.

After the year 1750 "The Messiah" was performed at least once annually during Handel's lifetime under his own direction in the chapel of the Foundling Hospital for the benefit of that institution, to which he bequeathed a set of orchestral parts. Handel himself conducted "The Messiah" thirty-four times. At the last performance at which he was announced to appear, on May 3, 1759, and which was given notwithstanding his death, which occurred on April 14th, the orchestra consisted of twelve first and second violins, three violas, three 'cellos, two double basses, four oboes, four bassoons, two horns, two trumpets, kettledrums, clavichord, and organ, while the chorus numbered five principals (two women and three men), six boys, and twelve adult choristers. This body Handel had considered sufficient for producing

the required effects in a hall capable of seating
about a thousand persons. The distribution
of the instruments of the orchestra represents
the then customary proportions between the
strings and the oboes and bassoons, by which
they were reinforced in the full passages.
These proportions were : one oboe to about
three violins, one bassoon to each 'cello, and
another to each double bass. The manner in
which the reinforcements were to be employed
was minutely indicated by Handel in the score
and parts.

Such was the popularity of " The Messiah,"
for many years the only oratorio which it was
customary to give complete, that it opened
a new era in choral culture in England and
called into life the Handel cult which has
not died out to the present day. The Lenten
performances organised by Handel were carried on by John Christopher Smith (1712–1795),
Handel's former amanuensis, and John Stan-
ley (1713–1786). These led up to the great
Handel celebration which took place in commemoration of the centenary of Handel's birth,
in Westminster Abbey and the Pantheon from
May 26 to June 5, 1784 (a year too early for
the centenary festival), and which the historian
Burney has so attractively described. On this
occasion the chorus, including the principals,

numbered two hundred and seventy-five, divided into : sixty sopranos, of whom forty-seven
were boys ; forty-eight altos, all men ; eighty-
three tenors; and eighty-four basses. The orchestra numbered two hundred and fifty. It
is noteworthy that notwithstanding such a relation between the vocalists and instrumentalists, Abbé Vogler (1749–1814), a remarkably
versatile musician who contrived to obtain
notoriety in England and on the Continent by
his eccentricities as well as by his talents,
pronounced the chorus too powerful for the
orchestra.

The fitness of Handel's music for performance on a grand scale having been demonstrated, Handel festivals became of common occurrence. In Germany Johann Adam Hiller
(1728–1804), a most active choral and orchestral conductor, imitated the example set at
London by giving " The Messiah," in an Italian
translation, in the Cathedral at Berlin in May,
1786, with a chorus of one hundred and eighteen and an orchestra of one hundred and
eighty-six. Hiller did not hesitate to pander
to public taste and to the vanity of the principal soloist by interpolating an Italian aria.
He also attempted to modernise Handel's
work by rewriting the parts for the wind instruments and making changes in the letter

of the music. So little reverence was entertained at the time for " The Messiah " in Germany that the advisability of composing new arias for the oratorio was openly discussed.

It was in the nature of such festivals that efforts should have been made to increase the sonority of the orchestral volume in keeping with that of the constantly growing vocal body; and as this could be most readily accomplished by the introduction of additional wind and particularly brass instruments, Handel oratorios were subjected to all sorts of deplorable indignities for the sake of producing noise merely,—a practice which has unfortunately survived to the present day.

In striking contrast with such innovations are the additional accompaniments which Mozart wrote in 1789 at the request of Baron van Swieten for several of Handel's oratorios, among them "The Messiah," in order to make their performance possible without the help of an organ. The manner in which he did this has met with the unqualified approval and has challenged the admiration of the most critical. Even the purists who would restore the original, to modern taste, unsatisfactory instrumentation cannot deny that Mozart's version has brought " The Messiah " nearer to the understanding and sympathies of the people without in any way doing violence to the composer's intentions. Robert Franz, having discovered that the score attributed to Mozart contained much that had come neither from Mozart's nor Handel's pen, in 1884 published an edition of " The Messiah," critically revised on the basis of the best manuscripts, in which all gaps in instrumentation are filled out and a number of carefully considered alterations appear.

The acme of extraordinary performances of Handel's works has been reached at the Handel Festivals which were begun in 1857 at the Crystal Palace, Sydenham, under the auspices of the London Sacred Harmonic Society, then conducted by Sir Michael Costa (1810–1884), and which have been held triennially with one exception since 1862. On some of these occasions over three thousand singers have been assembled and an orchestra of five hundred has been gathered together. The numerical relation between the vocal and instrumental forces has therefore been brought into accord with modern ideas. In the Triennial Festival of the current year, which took place in June, four thousand performers participated. As such undertakings seldom yield artistic results and are necessarily confined to the production of the best known of Handel's oratorios, they add little to the knowledge of his works, a goodly number of which have undeservedly been permitted to become obsolete, notwithstanding the fact that, especially when discriminately pruned, they can be made effective.

VII

Other Choral Forms

OF the attempts made in England to pursue the course marked out for the oratorio by Handel, whose works were there estimated at their true value, none succeeded in attracting more than passing interest. In Germany the Italian operatic oratorio ruled supreme, Bach's influence remaining purely local for many decades. In the meanwhile Gluck (1714–1787) was liberating the drama from the technical mannerisms of tyrannous singers, Haydn (1732–1809) was shaping the symphony, and Mozart (1756–1791) was pouring forth floods of glowing, pulsating melody, and enriching the orchestral pallet. When, therefore, Haydn in 1795, at the age of sixty-three, began to compose "The Creation," he had at his service vocal and instrumental forms and means of musical expression of which even he could have had but a faint conception at the time of writing his Italian oratorio, "The Return of Tobias," twenty-four years before.

Haydn was persuaded to undertake the composition of "The Creation" and "The Seasons" by Baron von Swieten, to whom the musical circles of Vienna owed their acquaintance with Handel's "Messiah," and who provided the aged composer with the text-books, which he had translated and adapted—that of "The Creation" from a poem by Lidley, based on Milton's "Paradise Lost," that of "The Seasons" from a poem by J. Thomson. For the composition of "The Creation" which, it is said, gave Haydn much trouble, Von Swieten and his coterie of musical friends guaranteed Haydn five hundred florins, about two hundred dollars. Under their care the first performance of the oratorio took place at the Schwarzenberg palace, Vienna, before an invited audience on April 29, 1798. In public it was produced for the first time on March 19th of the following year at the National Theatre under the auspices of the same patrons, who defrayed all the expenses and handed over to the composer the entire proceeds, amounting to four thousand florins.

The poem of "The Creation" is not a dramatic one, as the personages introduced appear as narrators only. This very fact was to the advantage of Haydn, the trend of whose genius was purely lyric, for it left him un-

trammelled to give free rein to his exuberant
fancy and create the series of pictures and
scenes which for loveliness of sentiment, descriptive beauty, and grace have never been
excelled. To the orchestral movements and
the illustrative accompaniments Haydn devoted particular care, for this was his own peculiar sphere. A striking example of felicitous
orchestration is to be found in "Raphael's"
(bass) narrative of the sixth day : the creation
of animal life, which is so rich in imitative bits
of tone painting that it has become known
among singers as the "zoological aria." Notwithstanding its picturesqueness and occasional
realism Haydn's music always remains poetic
and beautiful and is exalted by an all-pervading
childlike, joyful, religious enthusiasm. In construction the choruses of "The Creation"
show the influence of Handel, whose oratorios
Haydn had carefully studied and had heard in
Vienna and London, though in power and dramatic spirit they fall short of those of that
master of choral effects.

Even less organically connected than the
scenes of "The Creation" are those of "The
Seasons," which constitute a series of cantatas
rather than an oratorio. They concern themselves with human happenings and appealed to
Haydn's sympathies for folk-life, with which

he was in close touch, and which he was particularly fond of picturing.

"The Seasons" too was produced for the first time at the Schwarzenberg palace, on April 24, 1801. "Astonishment alternated with loudly expressed enthusiasm among the hearers" wrote a chronicler of this notable event.

The strain imposed on the venerable Haydn's vitality by the composition of "The Seasons," which was begun shortly after the completion of "The Creation," proved too great. His strength of body and happiness of mind failed him little by little. He appeared for the last time in public at a performance of "The Creation" given on March 27, 1808, by the "Musical Society of Dilettanti" with an orchestra of sixty and a chorus of only thirty-two under the direction of Salieri (1750–1825), a celebrated operatic composer and conductor. When the chorus burst forth with the words "And there was light," Haydn profoundly agitated exclaimed, pointing toward Heaven, "It came from thence!"—words which offer the best commentary on the spirit in which he had conceived this master-work. A little more than a year later Haydn expired.

The influence of Haydn's "Creation" on the development of choral culture in Germany was as puissant as had been that of Handel's

" Messiah " in England. Choral societies were
organised in cities, towns, and villages for the
special purpose of producing the new oratorio,
which on account of its easily comprehended
beauties and the comparative simplicity of its
choruses, was particularly adapted to the limited capabilities of inexperienced singers. The
demand created by these associations for similar works called forth a large number of them.
Descriptive and illustrative oratorios appeared
in profusion. The output of Haydn's imita-
tors, however, was so insignificant in quality
that its very existence is now forgotten.

Even before Beethoven (1770–1827) had entirely emancipated himself from the limitations
of formalism and had created the marvellously
eloquent musical vocabulary with the aid of
which he subsequently gave such direct and
forceful expression to the most intense human
emotions and the most varied moods, he wrote
a choral work which is as remarkable for its
musical charm as for the boldness with which it
defies all religious traditions. This work, "The
Mount of Olives," which is classed sometimes
with Passions, sometimes with oratorios, and
sometimes with sacred operas, Beethoven composed in 1803. Notwithstanding its obvious
incongruities, for which the text-book is largely
responsible, and the most glaring of which are

a scene and aria assigned to the Saviour, and a duet and trio in which the Saviour is joined by an angel and by an angel and St. Peter respectively, it was received with enthusiasm when first produced on April 5, 1803, in the Theater an der Wien, at Vienna, and after its publication in 1810 was quite generally performed throughout Germany. An unsuccessful attempt to rid Beethoven's music of its objectionable libretto was made in England in 1842 by Dr. Hudson of Dublin, who substituted for the original words a text founded on the story of David's sojourn in the wilderness. In this form it is known under the title "Engedi."

The romantic movement in music which laid more stress on the clear, definite, and picturesque expression in tones of emotions, fancies, and mental concepts than on the creation of works beautiful as to purely musical content and form, was not without influence on the oratorio. Among those who in sympathy with this tendency devoted themselves to the composition of oratorios Frederic Schneider (1786–1853) and Louis Spohr (1784–1859) attained prominence. The former's oratorio "The Judgment of the World," completed in 1819, created wide-spread but passing interest; the latter's "The Last Judgment" (Die letzten Dinge), produced for the first time at the Rhenish Festival of 1826, became particularly popular in England, where it is still in favour. These, not to mention less distinguished contemporaneous oratorio writers, were completely eclipsed by Felix Mendelssohn Bartholdy (1809–1847), who with " St. Paul " and " Elijah " recorded triumphs comparable only to those achieved by Handel with " The Messiah " and Haydn with " The Creation."

The popular success of Mendelssohn's oratorios was due to the fact that notwithstanding his sincere effort to combine the devotional depth of Bach with the brilliant power of Handel, the methods of both of whom he had thoroughly assimilated, he remained true to his own style, which in its suave beauty and calm fervour was within the ready comprehension of his time and in harmony with its emotional and imaginative tendencies. Less profound than Bach and less virile than Handel, he entertained sentiments and formed conceptions of the characters to be portrayed, which were in perfect accord with the somewhat sentimental religious life of his day. Possessed of all the resources of musical expression and illustration which had been developed since Haydn, he was enabled to give utterance to these sentiments and to realise these conceptions in a musical language which appealed directly to his hearers, but which, as it was always choice, was not harmful to musical taste.

It admits of little doubt that as a composer Mendelssohn was somewhat overrated during his lifetime. This was largely due to his remarkably sympathetic personality, his superior gifts of mind and comprehensive education, and to his many-sided public activity ; for he was one of the most refined of the pianists then living, an organist unexcelled in the art of extemporising, and a conductor of great technical ability and of irresistible magnetism. Equally certain is it that Mendelssohn is now underrated ; for after all has been said that can be justly brought forward against his best works, and " Elijah " is one of them, the fact remains that they are rich in melody, are constructed with consummate contrapuntal skill and knowledge of choral effects, orchestrated with rare taste, and that in point of form they fall little short of perfection. As Mendelssohn could not but yield to his extraordinary faculty of inventing sensuously charming melodies, his lyric utterances are often devoid of forcefulness, the absence of which is more keenly felt since the dramatic spirit and dramatic methods have asserted themselves in every class of musical composition. That he was capable, however, of strong characterisation and was a master in adapting

MENDELSSOHN.

the polyphonic forms—the ideal forms for extended choral movements—to the expression of intensely emotional states and to the requirements of dramatic situations, a number of scenes in " Elijah " show, for they are sufficiently dramatic both in conception and execution to admit of performance on the stage. In point of fluency and effectiveness Mendelssohn's choral style has not been surpassed, if it has been equalled, by any other modern composer.

Although Mendelssohn conceived the idea of writing an oratorio as a favourite project before he was twenty years of age, he did not venture on such an undertaking until urged by the Cecilia Society of Frankfort-on-the-Main to compose an oratorio with St. Paul for its subject. Unable to come to an understanding with Professor Bernhard Marx (1799–1866), lecturer on music at the Berlin University, in regard to the introduction of the chorale, Mendelssohn compiled the text-book himself from the Bible with the assistance of two friends. With the composition of the music he was occupied at intervals from 1834 to 1836. In the meanwhile the right of producing it for the first time was acquired for the Lower Rhenish Festival of 1836, the Cecilia Society having been compelled to renounce its claim on the work in consequence of the illness of its director. Accordingly the first performance of "St. Paul" took place on May 22d of that year at Düsseldorf, under the direction of the composer. As an amusing incident of this concert it is related that when one of the " False Witnesses " failed to take up his cue, Fanny, Mendelssohn's sister, who sang in the chorus, averted disastrous consequences by humming his part and setting him aright. The oratorio was received with unprecedented enthusiasm ; yet Mendelssohn having detected shortcomings in design and details subjected it to a thorough revision, cutting out as many as ten numbers. " St. Paul " was seized upon with such eagerness by choral societies that in Germany alone one hundred and fifty performances of it were recorded within eighteen months of the Düsseldorf production.

From the importance which Mendelssohn assigned to the chorale in " St. Paul " it is evident that he planned this oratorio with Bach's Passions in mind. While such a scheme offered obvious advantages for contriving beautiful musical effects, it was inconsistent for an oratorio, and encouraged the already wide-spread inclination to confuse the form of the oratorio with that of the Passion or mystery.

The results of the ten years of study, reflection, and experience following the production of "St. Paul" are embodied in "Elijah," the work which marks the culmination of Mendelssohn's creative activity. The choice of this subject is said to have been determined by the passage "Behold, the Lord passeth by," which appealed forcibly to Mendelssohn's imagination and subsequently inspired him to a most picturesque choral setting. His principal aim in compiling the text was to make it as coherently dramatic as possible. The sequel proved that he was wise in so doing, for, although "Elijah" like "St. Paul" consists of a series of detached scenes, those of the former oratorio gain force by revolving about one central figure, while those of the latter suffer by being connected inferentially only. In the characterisation of that central figure and in the description of the miraculous occurrences with which it is identified in the narrative, Mendelssohn most eloquently demonstrated his resourcefulness in choral and orchestral composition.

The first production of "Elijah" took place at the Birmingham Festival of 1846 on the morning of August 26th, at the Town Hall. The orchestra numbered one hundred and twenty-five and the chorus two hundred and seventy-one, the sixty altos of which were men—Mendelssohn called them his "bearded altos." When Mendelssohn appeared on the stage he was greeted by the vast audience, which had taken possession of all the available space, with deafening applause, in which the orchestra and chorus joined. Then amid the quiet of anxious expectancy the performance began. The astonishment of the hearers when after a few introductory chords Staudigl, the great German bass, who sang the titular part, announced the prophecy in the impressive recitative which precedes the overture, can scarcely be imagined. For such a bold innovation few were prepared, and its effect must, therefore, have been overpowering.

According to Mendelssohn's own testimony none other of his works was hailed with such enthusiasm by musicians and the public as " Elijah." Nevertheless he thoroughly revised this oratorio, too, abbreviating, rewriting, and rescoring. The trio for women's voices, " Lift thine eyes," which has become so universally popular, was one of the results of this revision. The original setting of the words was for two voices only.

Numerous efforts have been made and are constantly making, on the one hand, to apply to the principles observed by Mendelssohn in the oratorio the methods which have revolutionised the modern lyric drama, on the other, to evolve new constructive principles on the basis of these methods. None of these efforts has so far been conspicuously successful, and it remains to be seen whether the fusion of such apparently incompatible elements is possible in the choral oratorio.

In England, where the exceptional facilities offered by the regularly recurring festivals for the production of large choral works act as a constant stimulus to composers, the contributions to oratorio literature have been most copious. Yet in that country Mendelssohn's influence has remained particularly powerful and is but thinly veiled by the profuse employment of the modern resources of musical composition.

In "The Redemption," produced for the first time at the Birmingham Festival of 1882, Charles François Gounod (1818–1893) attempted to create a new type of religious music which he described as "plane music and music painted in fresco." The morbidly mystic character of this work, the plan of which is framed after that of Bach's Passions, is only emphasised by the composer's analytical exposition of the symbolical nature of the tone structure.

Directly antipodal to this type in purpose and style are the oratorios or sacred operas of Anton Rubinstein (1829–1894), "Paradise Lost," "The Tower of Babel," "Moses," and "Christ," to the full effect of which imaginary if not real scenic environment is necessary. The two last mentioned are in fact Biblical operas intended for representation on a specially constructed stage. Such a production of "Christ," prepared on a most elaborate scale according to the instructions and under the supervision of Rubinstein, took place at Bremen in 1895, several months after his death, without, however, inviting imitation.

Remarkable for eclecticism and for the utter unconstraint with which the composer has utilised different styles and forms of vocal and instrumental music, sacred and secular, are the oratorios "The Legend of St. Elizabeth" and "Christ," by Franz Liszt (1811–1886). The "Legend of St. Elizabeth" was composed to celebrate the dedication of the restored Wartburg, the scene of the singing contest of the minnesingers in Wagner's "Tannhäuser," and Luther's asylum from 1521 to 1522. It was suggested by the frescoes then newly painted on the walls of the Wartburg by Moritz von Schwind, which represent scenes from the life of St. Elizabeth. In attempting to reproduce these scenes Liszt made extensive use of typical phrases, taken in part from a hymn sung in the sixteenth century on the festival of St. Elizabeth, which he elaborated with all possible skill and presented in a kaleidoscopic profusion of orchestral tone colours. In " Christ," likewise a series of detached scenes, plain chant melodies, Latin Church hymns, and mediæval spiritual songs in varied settings touch elbows with high-tinted orchestral tone paintings of the most realistic kind.

Among more recent contributions to the literature of the oratorio may be mentioned " St. Francis" by Edgar Tinel (1854–), in which the diversity of styles is even more crassly accentuated than in Liszt's " St. Elizabeth " ; and the unduly heralded Passion-trilogy and oratorios by Don Lorenzo Perosi (1872–), in which an attempt is made at the combination of mediæval and modern methods.

These are a few of the works in which the efforts to discover new paths in the composition of the choral oratorio in its most comprehensive sense are most plainly in evidence. Such efforts have not as yet yielded any far-reaching results, for they have not added anything of grandeur and impressiveness to the polyphonic style so well suited to the choral oratorio, or supplanted it with one more forceful or better adapted to the character of that form. Until they shall have accomplished one or the other of these ends they must be characterised as tentative only.

As music emancipated itself from the ritualistic constraint of the Church, composers were not slow to realise the opportunities offered by the missal text for the construction of elaborate accompanied choral works.

At the very dividing line between music of and for the Church and music independent of such environment stands Bach's stupendous mass in B minor, in which the composer gave utterance to his conception of the religious significance of the words without considerations of any kind save those imposed by his own devotional feeling and his musical sensibilities. The result was one of the greatest choral works of all times, and one which, notwithstanding its marvellously intricate construction, appeals directly to the hearer on account of the lofty beauty and the plastic contours of its themes and of the illustrative character of some of its movements. Bach wrote the first two parts of the mass in 1733 for the royal chapel at Dresden and dedicated them to the Elector of Saxony with the request for an honorary title, which he coveted to offset the slights offered him by the authorities of Leipsic, to whom he was subordinate as cantor. The remaining movements he did not complete until five years later.

Haydn and Mozart in their masses (excepting the latter's Requiem) made little effort to improve on the operatic style cultivated in the churches of Austria at the time.

Almost entirely dissociated from any ecclesiastical purport is Beethoven's great mass in D, the only mass which can in any way be compared with Bach's. When Beethoven in 1818 began the composition of this, his second mass, he had in mind the ceremony which was to signalise the installation of his distinguished patron, the Archduke of Austria, as Archbishop of Olmütz; but before he had got well under way with it his inspiration was not to be checked. The movements outgrew all practicable proportions, and the score, instead of being completed within the two years originally allotted, was not finished until four years had passed. Beethoven devoted himself to this task with all the impetuosity of his volcanic nature. According to Schindler, his friend and biographer, he at times fell into a state of uncontrollable excitement while at work, pacing the floor, stamping, shouting, and singing like one possessed.

Beethoven looked at the text of the mass not in the light of its liturgical significance but in that of its poetical suggestiveness. His setting of it is therefore intensely emotional and imaginative, and in places even picturesquely dramatic, as witness the much discussed trumpet fanfares accompanied by drums in the " Agnus Dei," which serve to throw into relief the prayer for peace by suggesting the tumult of battle.

This monumental work literally went a-begging. A circular soliciting subscribers for the score addressed to all the European courts brought only seven favourable replies, among which was one offering a royal order in place of the subscription price of fifty ducats (about one hundred and twenty-five dollars)—a proposition which Beethoven, who was in need of money, indignantly rejected. He was not even permitted to hear a complete performance of the mass. It was at St. Petersburg in 1824 that such a one was made possible through the efforts of Prince Galitzin. In Vienna only single movements, with the text translated into German, were given during Beethoven's lifetime under the name of " hymns," owing to the interference of the censor.

Of greater attractiveness than the solemn mass to composers who were under the spell of imaginative and descriptive music, was the mass for the dead, the Requiem, particularly on account of the opportunities for the introduction of unusual orchestral effects offered by the sequence " Dies Iræ." In this field François Joseph Gossec (1733–1829) proved a pioneer. His mass for the dead performed at St.

Roch in 1760 created a sensation, principally on account of the " Tuba mirum," written for two orchestras, one of wind instruments concealed outside the church, and one of strings placed within it, which accompanied the former *pianissimo* and *tremolo* in the highest registers. This innovation, however, appears innocuous when compared with Berlioz's (1803–1869) theatrical attempt to picture the terrors of the judgment day by adding to the full orchestra sixteen drums with ten players and four brass bands stationed in different parts of the church. By the side of such an array of instruments the requirements of Verdi's (1813–) gorgeously coloured Requiem are modest indeed. Notwithstanding the absence of any adventitious means Mozart's Requiem excels such works by far in tenderness, pathos, and real force.

One of the most noble, dignified, and heartfelt choral compositions of recent times is " A German Requiem " by Johannes Brahms (1833–1897), a series of deeply contemplative movements on Scriptural selections treating of death, eternity, and the happiness of the life to come, in which all the resources of modern harmony, counterpoint, and orchestration are employed with consummate skill and refined taste.

Among the excerpts from the Roman ritual which have invited musical treatment in the smaller forms are the sequence, "Stabat Mater," the Ambrosian hymn of praise, " Te Deum," and the song of the Virgin Mary, " Magnificat." Prominent among the settings of these, which are really sacred cantatas, are: the profound one by Bach of the Magnificat ; the virile and brilliant Utrecht and Dettingen Te Deum by Handel, the fantasic Te Deum by Berlioz, composed as a part of a projected ceremony commemorative of Napoleon I. ; and the several settings of the Stabat Mater by Emanuel Astorga (1681–1736); by Giovanni Pergolesi (1710–1736) ; by Rossini (1792–1868)—a glaring illustration of the misapplication of extraordinary musical gifts—and the individually characteristic Stabat Mater by Antonin Dvořák (1841–).

Although the oratorio is not necessarily limited to the treatment of sacred subjects, as the secular oratorios of Handel and Haydn demonstrate, tradition has assigned to it such a circumscribed sphere and a correspondingly reserved and elevated style. In order to escape such restrictions modern composers have either refrained from classifying their choral works at all or have adopted for them new, more or less accurate, designations, as, for instance, dramatic legend, dramatic cantata, dramatic or lyric scenes, choral ballad, and poem, according to the larger or smaller dimensions of the composition and its predominatingly dramatic, narrative, descriptive or contemplative character.

As notable examples of such works may be instanced Mendelssohn's charmingly illustrative "Walpurgis Night"; Schumann's (1810–1856) melodious "Paradise and the Peri," and meditative "Scenes from Faust" (particularly the mystic third part); Berlioz's demoniac "Faust"; the picturesque "Song of Destiny" and the forceful "Song of Triumph" by Brahms; and Dvořák's realistic "The Spectre's Bride." In England the output of compositions of this class, stimulated by the needs of the provincial festivals, has been very large. Among those which of recent times have attracted unusual attention on account of their signalising departures from the well-beaten path, may be mentioned S. Coleridge Taylor's (1875–) spontaneously melodic, though somewhat reiterative scenes from Longfellow's "The Song of Hiawatha" and Edward William Elgar's (1857–) contemplative and intricately constructed settings of portions of Cardinal Newman's "The Dream of Gerontius" (Birmingham Festival of 1900).

With so great a variety of forms to choose from, composers are perfectly free to resort to any methods which may best suit their purposes; and as conciseness and directness of expression are at present held to be of more importance than beauty of musical content and workmanship, the methods they preferably employ are not such as are peculiar to the highly organised contrapuntal types, the types which have been hitherto considered as most intimately in accord with the genius of choral music. As a consequence the choral style is losing much of its individuality and is yielding more and more to the influence of modern instrumental music—a result which is to be deplored as long as the harm it brings to refined chorus singing is not offset by advantages of unquestionably artistic significance.

VIII

Amateur Choral Culture in Germany and England

NOTWITHSTANDING the interest in chorus singing which such institutions as the choruses of alumni and students created in Germany, it was not until the end of the eighteenth century that circumstances arose favourable to the organisation of choral societies independent of the Church and the school on the one hand and of the opera on the other. Up to the middle of that century musical activity, productive and reproductive, revolved about one or the other of these two centres. Music was composed either for lending impressiveness to the devotional exercises of the people or for adding lustre to the entertainments of royalty and the aristocracy. It was performed either by specially trained church choirs or by royal and private chapels. As an art sufficient unto itself, independent of such purposes, music was scarcely recognised. Public concerts were of rare occurrence, and it is sig-

nificant that the few which took place should
have consisted in oratorio performances, with
and without scenery and action, and in " oratorios," as miscellaneous concerts too were universally called, given merely to provide a substitute for operatic representations, which were
prohibited during Lent as well as on all great
church festivals.   To this class belonged the
spiritual concerts founded by Anne Danican-
Philidor (1681–1728) in 1725 at Paris, the Lent-
en oratorio concerts permanently organised by
Handel in 1739 in London, and those established at Vienna in 1772 by the Association of
Musical Artists.

The dearth of public musical entertainments
acted as an incentive for amateurs to meet
together for the practice of concerted music.
Such gatherings, as has been shown, were heartily encouraged by the conductors of church
choirs, and in some cases led up to the establishment of permanent concert institutions.   The
society of students, for instance, which assembled every week at a tavern in Leipsic to sing
and play, and the direction of which Bach
assumed in 1736, gave the impulse to the formation of the association out of which the "Gewandhaus" concerts ultimately grew.

Such associations — dilettanti associations
they were called, and their entertainments, di-

lettanti concerts, in contradistinction to the professional concerts—became more and more numerous as singers and instrumentalists increased in number and efficiency and as under the influence of Haydn, Mozart, and Beethoven music became independent of the Church and the stage. For a time social elements entered very largely into their meetings. A supper and dance almost invariably followed the musical programme, which was only too often arranged with a view towards providing opportunity for the display of the attainments of individuals. For these and similar reasons many of the societies were short-lived. With those that survived, however, the musical features became of paramount importance and attained to a certain degree of artistic dignity. In some instances most rigid rules looking towards such results were framed. The statutes of a society of dilettanti established at Heilbronn in 1785, for example, prohibited eating, drinking, and smoking at its entertainments, and provided for the exclusion of incorrigible chatterers and for the prevention of interruption or disturbance of the performances.

Similar institutions were organised by the nobility and aristocracy when towards the middle of the eighteenth century many of the royal and princely chapels were dissolved. The titled classes of Austria and Bohemia especially, rendered invaluable services to the cause of music by promoting worthy performances of the choral master-works. In order to make these possible they not only contributed the necessary pecuniary means but gave active assistance as well in the ranks of the orchestra and chorus. Under such circumstances the productions of Handel's oratorios begun by Baron von Swieten, for which Mozart wrote his additional accompaniments, took place at Vienna from 1788 to 1790, and those of Haydn's " Creation " in 1799, and of " The Seasons " in 1801.

The members of the nobility lent the prestige of their patronage to such enterprises even when undertaken by the upper middle classes, and occasionally went so far as to participate in them—a proof of devotion to the musical art greater than which they could not give, and an indication of the growth of appreciation of its dignity and of the respect due to its exponents.

To the dilettanti concerts, which were not supposed to be subject to public criticism, at least in the early stages of the movement, subscribers only were admitted, who paid merely a nominal sum for this privilege. As very few concerts were given outside of these—in Vienna, for instance, only four during the whole season—there was no lack of patrons. Indeed, it was a cause of constant complaint that even for visitors from other cities it was impossible to obtain admission to such entertainments.

The dilettanti concerts were incapable of a high degree of development because of the absence of lofty aims and of an artistic standard. Symphonies were played without any rehearsals, and oratorios with the most insufficient preparation. The fact that in the small town of Stettin it was customary to rehearse a programme three or four times was made the subject of laudatory comment in a public journal of Berlin, coupled with the humiliating confession that in the Prussian capital not even a single full rehearsal could be counted upon. Nevertheless these associations served a good purpose. To quote the keen critic Eduard Hanslick—" They did not, as they perhaps hoped, make the whole population musical, but certainly themselves."

The dilettanti concerts were doomed as soon as professional orchestral associations established themselves, which elevated instrumental performances to a point beyond the reach of amateurs. These educated the public to demand in choral music, too, which was dependent on the co-operation of non-professionals, a degree of efficiency to be attained by systematic practice only, and up to the end of the eighteenth century the necessity of systematic practice had not been thought of among amateurs.

So far as the question of the permanent organisation of bodies of amateur singers desirous of devoting themselves seriously to the study of choral music is concerned, regardless of the immediate artistic results achieved, America seems to have the right of claiming priority, as will be shown in the chapter following. The first society, however, destined to accomplish the results which revolutionised choral culture by showing that artistic achievements were possible with larger numbers of amateur singers, was the Singakademie of Berlin, founded in 1790; and the man who devised the methods by means of which this was effected was Karl Christian Fasch (1736-1800).

This admirably equipped and earnest-minded musician, after having acted in companionship with Philipp Emanuel Bach (1714-1788) as accompanist to the royal flutist Frederick the Great of Prussia, for almost twenty years, removed to Berlin for the purpose of giving vocal lessons and devoting himself to the composition of unaccompanied choral music in the mediæval style. In 1783 Reichardt (1752-1814), the royal chapel-master, submitted to Fasch for

FASCH.

examination the score of a mass in sixteen parts by Orazio Benevoli (1602–1672), a celebrated Italian contrapuntist. Fasch, seized with the desire to outdo the Italian master, set about writing a similar mass under the additional self-imposed restriction of grouping the voices into four independent choruses, and applied himself to the task with such persistence as to bring on a hemorrhage of the lungs. Longing to hear his work he attempted its performance at first with twenty of the royal choristers in Potsdam and then with members of the church choir. The results were so distressing that Fasch was compelled to lay aside his mass unheard for a time at least.

In the meanwhile several young women had joined the circle of his pupils, among them the daughter and stepdaughter of the Privy Councillor Milow, who, appreciative of the pleasure and benefit to be derived from the practice of concerted music, persuaded her fellow-students and a few friends to form a little choir, which Fasch was requested to instruct. Fasch became deeply interested in this activity, largely because it promised to afford him an opportunity to hear his own works. In 1790 the meetings assumed the character of regular rehearsals and were held in the summer-house of the Privy Councillor. They were attended by from twelve to sixteen persons, members of the leading families of Berlin. Discontinued during the winter, they were resumed the following spring, and on May 27, 1791, when the first record of attendance was kept, twenty-seven singers answered to their names. This is the date which is celebrated as that of the foundation of the "Singakademie," the name subsequently adopted for the society.

Neither Fasch nor any one of the little band which was gathered about him in 1790 had in view the establishment of a permanent association, least of all did he dream that he was taking the first step in a movement which would create a revolution in choral culture. All were animated by the one object of self-improvement, the one incentive of love for music, the one ambition of doing justice to an undertaken task. Unlike the members of the dilettanti societies, they studied choral works not for the sake of deriving and affording amusement, but for the purpose of broadening their knowledge and refining their taste. Actuated by such motives and guided by a conductor of high ideals, of skill, and practical sense, they could not but accomplish results which in the course of time attracted wide-spread attention—though this was not of their seeking—and enlisted the active interest even of professional musicians. To the

perpetuation of such a spirit and of such conditions it is due that the Singakademie has survived to the present day and has remained a
strong factor in the promotion of choral culture.

In 1793, the membership of the society having increased to forty-three and outgrown the
capacity of the rooms which could be placed at
its disposal in private houses, permission to
meet in the Royal Academy of Science and
Art was obtained. Fasch now suggested a plan
of organisation, which was adopted. He appointed a board of three men and three women
on whom devolved the administrative duties of
the society. Over its musical conduct he retained absolute control. To defray the necessary current expenses each member contributed twelve groschen, about twenty-five cents,
a month. Professional musicians were exempt
from the payment of dues, on the ground that
they lent their services to the loss of valuable
time. Fasch not only officiated as conductor
without any remuneration, but composed constantly for the choir, and even copied the necessary number of parts of the works to be studied. The great mass of manuscripts in his
handwriting which are preserved in the library
of the society bears testimony to his self-sacrificing industry.

Scarcely less zealous than their director were

the members of the society. In these days
when chorus singers labour under the impression that in attending rehearsals they are be-
stowing rather than receiving benefits, it seems
strange to read that on a stormy and cold night
when the meeting-room on account of inade-
quate facilities for heating was so chilly as to
endanger health, the women of the Singakademie, unwilling to cut short the rehearsal,
knelt down so as to be able to cover their feet
with their cloaks, and in this attitude held out
to the end of the study hour.

Although the original object of the society
was to cultivate chorus singing for the benefit
of its own active members, it soon became impossible to resist the demands for occasional
public appearances. Accordingly, on April 8,
1794, a so-called "auditorium," a public rehearsal, was arranged, to which only a limited
number of hearers were invited, among them
being Prince Louis Ferdinand and other members of the royal court. Once a beginning was
made, it became customary to give several
entertainments of this kind every season. Not
only these but the regular rehearsals, too, were
so unique at the time and excited so much interest that the permission to attend them was
considered an extraordinary privilege. Even
Beethoven, while in Berlin on a visit in 1796,

did not disdain to be present at a rehearsal. So highly was he pleased with the singing of the choir that, to show his appreciation, he sat down at the piano and extemporised on themes from the pieces he had heard—they happened to be of Fasch's composition.

The first concert of the society to which the general public was admitted on payment of an entrance fee took place on October 8, 1800, in the Garrison Church, under the direction of Zelter (1758–1832), the successor of Fasch, who had died on August 3d previous. The chorus taking part numbered one hundred and fifteen, and the orchestra, consisting of members of the royal chapel, thirty-three. The work performed was Mozart's Requiem, chosen in memory of Fasch.

Notwithstanding the success of this and other subsequent public performances, the society continued to adhere to its original purpose of self-education. This was again emphatically set forth in the article of the revised constitution of 1817, which stated the object of the society to be the practice of music for the sake of study, and not with frequent public performances in view. To the absence of the spirit which dictated such a policy, and which ought to be the prevailing one in every chorus, is to be attributed the instability of singing societies, as they go. It was this same spirit that made it possible for Fasch to institute, and for his successor to continue, the thorough methods of training which earned for the Singakademie well-deserved fame. One of the most efficient of these was the organisation of a preparatory chorus in which less advanced singers could obtain the knowledge and experience requisite to their promotion to the main body.

The rate at which the Singakademie grew can be judged from the following figures. In 1794 the chorus numbered sixty-six; in 1795, eighty-four. In 1802 the membership reached two hundred; in 1813, three hundred, in 1827, four hundred, and in 1833, five hundred. Since 1880 the membership has hovered about six hundred.

Of the many proud achievements to which the Singakademie can point, the one which was perhaps of the greatest historical significance was the rescue from almost total oblivion of Bach's " Passion according to St. Matthew " by its performance in 1829 at the urgent solicitation and under the direction of Mendelssohn, then a lad of twenty.

Notwithstanding the brilliant example set by the Singakademie of Berlin, amateurs were slow to give up the superficial enjoyment afforded by the concerts of dilettanti for the more serious work required in well-organised societies. Nine years elapsed before another institution similar to the parent one was established, and up to 1818, twenty-seven years after the foundation of the Singakademie, only ten amateur singing societies were regularly active in Germany. After that time, however, they multiplied with great rapidity. Now there is scarcely a village or town without its chorus. Many of these rarely appear in public. They are conducted for the benefit and in the interest of the active members and a small circle of friends only.

The study at home of the works in rehearsal being rather the rule than the exception, the modern classics have become household possessions in Germany. Nor are the unaccompanied master works of the mediæval composers, Italian and German, neglected. Not a few institutions make their practice a specialty. These have admirable models in such professional bodies as the time-honoured choir of the church of St. Thomas at Leipsic, of which Bach was cantor from 1723 to 1750; and the cathedral choir of Berlin, which was founded in 1839 and permanently organised as a rival of the Sistine Chapel by command of Frederick IV., King of Prussia (1840–1861). Composed of about sixty members each, consisting

of boys (for the soprano and alto) carefully selected and perfectly trained, and of the most
competent men obtainable, and instructed by
musicians thoroughly versed in the traditions
of mediæval music, these choirs accomplish
results little short of perfect.

Although numerically imposing, German
male choruses have not contributed much towards choral culture in its highest aspect. Their
tendency is rather national, patriotic, and social than artistic, their sphere of musical activity circumscribed by their nature. Traceable
to the seventeenth century, these semi-social,
semi-musical clubs did not become popular
until Zelter, in 1808, organised the first " Lieder-
tafel " with twenty-four men from the Berlin
Singakademie. Stimulated by the wave of
patriotism which found such vigorous expression in Theodore Körner's (1791–1813) poems
and Carl Maria von Weber's (1786–1826) setting
of them, the number of these clubs increased
with amazing rapidity. Subsequently combined into one grand " Bund," they at intervals
unite to give a gigantic festival, " Sängerfest,"
" Bundesfest." In a celebration of this character held at Dresden in 1865, no fewer than
twenty thousand singers participated.

While some of the German male choruses
have brought part singing to a degree of per-

fection not often attained by mixed choirs, they cannot be considered a factor of importance to the development of choral culture on account of the necessarily limited artistic scope of the music at their disposal.

In England, the cradle and nursery of the choral oratorio, amateur mixed choruses were slower to be established permanently than in Germany. This is to be accounted for by the fact that church music remained in the exclusive charge of professional choirs of boys and men longer in the former than in the latter country. In Germany the music of the Protestant ritual, being less rigidly fixed than in England, admitted of a degree of simplification which brought it within the capability of the congregation entirely unaided, or assisted by such choirs only as could be supplied with the help of the currendani and amateurs. As has been shown, this led to the popularisation of choral practice and to the more or less compact organisation of choirs from which women were not necessarily excluded. In England, on the other hand, the ritual of the Established Church required the co-operation of trained choirs at the ceremonial, which did not admit of the participation of women. The professional character of these choirs was furthermore upheld by the extended activity which they found in the performance of sacred music in churches, theatres, and even public gardens, particularly during Lent; for public concerts open to everyone on the payment of an admission fee were instituted in England as early as 1670, long before they were established in Germany. In 1681 the first vocal concert without the usual accessories of ale and tobacco was given in a public concert-room built for the purpose in Villiers Street, London, and a little later the concerts of Thomas Britton (born about 1651), " the small coal man," at which coffee was dispensed at a penny a dish, were founded. While, then, there were ample opportunities for boys and men to cultivate chorus singing, women were debarred from that privilege by deeply rooted prejudice. That this prejudice should have yielded more easily in the provinces, where trained boys' voices were scarce, than in London and other large cities, where cathedral choirs were available, is natural. Particularly in the northern and midland counties chorus singing was cultivated by both sexes owing to the superior quality of the voices and the pronounced musical talent of the inhabitants. As late as 1832 the Sacred Harmonic Society of London, established in that year, was dependent on the aid of chorus singers from the north of

England whom it induced to take up their residence in the metropolis by finding employment for them in order to have them at hand for its concerts.

A strong impulse was given to the diffusion of choral culture in the provinces by the musical festivals, which in the course of time assumed dimensions and a degree of artistic importance in England as in no other country. Originally these festivals were nothing more than special church services arranged generally in the interest of some charity by several cathedral choirs conjointly. Among the earliest events of this kind were those fathered by " The Corporation of the Sons of Clergy," which was established in 1655 and incorporated by charter of Charles II., in 1678. They have taken place annually at St. Paul's, London, since 1697, without, however, attaining to musical significance. Of greater importance musically were the celebrations of St. Cecilia's day, for the more artistic conduct of which " The Musical Society " was organised at London in 1683, and similar associations were formed in the provinces about the same time. Among the poets who wrote odes for such occasions were Dryden and Congreve, and among the composers who furnished musical settings, Purcell and Blow. At the last regular Cecilian festival, held in London in 1703, the chorus numbered about thirty boys and as many men, and the orchestra about twenty-five.

Of similar origin but incalculably more influential were the "Festivals of the Three Choirs" of Gloucester, Worcester, and Hereford, which have lost nothing of their vitality with the lapse of time. These, too, had their incipience in choral services in which the choirs of the three mentioned towns participated and which in 1724 assumed the shape of annual meetings. They took place in each of the cities in rotation and comprised, besides the services, two evening concerts of secular music and oratorios, which were given with orchestral accompaniment in the shire hall. To attract public interest orchestral reinforcements were brought from London and the services of the vocal celebrities of the day secured, often at such expense that the outlay for the concerts exceeded the receipts. Significant of the excellence of the choirs in the northern counties was the announcement of the appearance at the festival of 1772 in Gloucester of the "celebrated chorus singers from Lancashire and the North of England led by Miss Radcliffe."

The influence of these meetings soon became

apparent in that increasing numbers of amateurs joined the clubs into which the choristers had organised themselves, for the purpose of studying the works to be performed, and acquired the taste for a higher class of music, requisite to the establishment of the amateur singing societies which now contribute a large contingent to the festival forces. In 1836 the festivals of the Three Choirs were extended to four days' duration, and on this plan they have been carried on since. It is a pleasure incidentally to record that at the meeting of 1899 at Worcester that admirable work " Hora Novissima," by Professor Horatio W. Parker (1863–) of Yale University, was sung, and in such a manner as to justify the composer, who officiated as conductor, in pronouncing the chorus equal to any he had heard on the Continent. The meetings of the Three Choirs have retained their original character in that the cathedral choirs of the three cities continue to constitute the nucleus of the chorus. As a consequence a number of boys are to be found among the sopranos and a number of men among the altos. At the festival of the current year twenty-three of the seventy-five sopranos were boys and twelve of the fifty-eight altos men.

By far the most important of the provincial festivals are those held triennially at Birmingham. These were begun in 1768 with a series of performances in St. Philip's Church and in the theatre on King Street for the benefit of the General Hospital. The concerts were followed by balls. The programme of the first meeting was made up substantially of works by Handel, " The Messiah " among them, and was given by a chorus of forty boys and men and an orchestra of twenty-five. As a concession to public taste, instrumental solos were introduced between the several parts of the oratorios with the exception of " The Messiah," which escaped such a fate. In 1802 the policy of strengthening the chorus by the engagement of singers from London, from the Lichfield and Worcester cathedral choirs, and of sopranos, again from Lancashire, was adopted. It was not until 1855 that a local choral association was permanently established. This done, the forces, now consisting of the Birmingham Amateur Association augmented by choristers from London, whence the orchestra, too, was taken, rapidly increased in numbers, so that in 1876 the chorus aggregated three hundred and ninety and the orchestra one hundred and thirty. The co-operation of boy sopranos and men altos was gradually dispensed with. At the festival of the present year the chorus was composed of one hundred and seven sopranos, eighty-one contraltos, seventy-six tenors, and eighty-seven basses. Of these all were paid for their services with the exception of twenty-one—a fact which largely accounts for the balance of the parts and the efficiency of the body. The orchestra numbered one hundred and twenty-one.

That the attainment of the highest possible measure of musical excellence is the one supreme object of the Birmingham meetings, and that to this object all other considerations, local and even national, must yield, was illustrated by the appointment, in 1885, of Hans Richter (1843), the celebrated Vienna conductor, to the permanent leadership. As a result they deservedly enjoy the reputation of being the most notable choral events of the present time, so that to have a work performed at a Birmingham festival or to take a prominent part in such a one is a highly coveted distinction. Pecuniarily, too, the meetings have been attended with remarkable success, having earned for the hospital funds more than half a million of dollars.

Besides stimulating the regularly recurring festivals, more or less long-lived, the Handel cult in England launched a large number of isolated celebrations during the last decades of the eighteenth century, which led up to the establishment of local choruses. In illustration

there may be instanced the first performance of
"The Messiah" ever given north of the Trent,
which took place at Halifax about 1766. The
chorus on this occasion consisted principally
of the parishioners of a Rev. Allott of Kirk-
heaton, trained by himself. Joah Bates, the
conductor of the London Handel Commemoration, directed the concert, and the leader
(principal violin) of the orchestra was no less
celebrated a man than Sir William Herschel, the
astronomer. To this initiative can be traced
the origin of a number of choral societies in
that section of the country. In most cases,
however, cathedral choirs formed the nuclei
of the festival choruses and the centres about
which amateurs clustered until they had become sufficiently skilled to rely upon themselves. Whenever women joined choruses it
was to sing the soprano part only. The alto
part was invariably given to the counter-tenors—a practice with which German musicians,
Mendelssohn and Spohr in particular, found
serious fault.

While the participation of women in the singing of accompanied works of the larger forms
was making headway in the provinces, in London choirs of boys and men held undisputed
sway. When Dr. Arne (1710–1778), the rival
of Handel, and composer of "Rule, Britannia,"

introduced female voices (probably sopranos only) into his oratorio " Judith " and performed it accordingly in 1773, he was considered a bold innovator.

Oratorios, excepting " The Messiah," which was seldom dismembered, were rarely given complete in London until the Cæcilian Society, instituted in 1785, and the Sacred Harmonic Society, founded in 1832, began their oratorio concerts about 1836. The programme of the usual Lenten oratorio performances, so called, were hotchpotchs of sacred and secular pieces.

The difficulties which the scarcity of trained women's voices occasioned to societies devoted to choral culture of the higher class in the metropolis, and which were not overcome until the middle of the present century, are illustrated by the fact that the Academy of Ancient Concerts, founded in 1710, of which Handel was a supporter, when deprived in 1734 of the help of the children of the Chapel Royal, passed through a whole season without any treble voices—a situation from which escape was possible only through the establishment of a school for the free instruction of boys in singing. Towards remedying such a state of affairs by popularising chorus singing, Dr. John Hullah (1812–1884) largely contributed when in 1841 he organised the movement to instruct school-teachers in the system of musical training successfully followed by Wilhelm (1771–1842), director-general of musical instruction in the schools of Paris. Whatever may be thought of this system of "mutual instruction," Hullah's efforts were undoubtedly timely and productive of far-reaching results, for within a period of twenty years, twenty-five thousand persons passed through his classes.

To-day England in point of choral culture is excelled by no other country. It has become pre-eminently a nation of chorus singers. Bodies of amateurs can be gathered together in almost any section of the British Empire, which can be trusted with singing on the spur of the moment, often from memory, the favourite oratorios of Handel, Haydn, and Mendelssohn. The works of modern composers are on that account not neglected; and although, as seems right and just, English composers receive the larger share of that encouragement which comes from the knowledge that the fruits of their labours will not be consigned unheard to libraries and store-rooms, the best musical products of other countries are not overlooked.

In the matter of giving choral festivals on a large scale England to-day holds the highest place. In no other country would it be possible with so little effort to assemble such masses of choristers capable of singing almost without rehearsals Handel's better known oratorios, as take part in the Handel festivals. And while the artistic value of such stupendous performances is not above suspicion, the fact that they are practicable speaks volumes for the faithfulness with which England has guarded the heritage of her adopted son.

IX

Amateur Choral Culture in America

WHEN, in 1620, the Pilgrim Fathers landed at Plymouth Rock, they brought with them a hatred of musical culture which has no parallel in history. The enmity of the early Christians towards pagan art was associated with the desire to give to the Church its own art, one different from that of the pagans, but the enmity of the Pilgrim Fathers was directed against the musical art as such, and against anything and everything that could tend to foster it. That music in New England should have not only recovered from the blows dealt by Puritan intolerance but in its reproductive branches, and particularly that of chorus singing, should have risen to a certain degree of artistic independence as quickly as it did, is little short of marvellous.

When the eighteen years of the Great Rebellion in England (from 1642 to 1660), during which under Puritan fanaticism choruses were banished from the churches, music-books burned, and organs destroyed, had passed, enough of love and taste for music had survived to make possible the early reinstatement of cathedral service ; and although the character of church music was lowered by the introduction of the operatic style, rapid progress was made in the practice of the vocal and instrumental art. In New England, where the Puritan power remained supreme, no such reaction could take place; innate love of culture and of refinement was the only agency which could be counted upon to bring about the reformation necessary to musical development. The presence of this agency soon manifested itself by giving rise to a controversy which was carried on for more than a century.

The question as to whether singing should be allowed at all at divine service was more quickly disposed of than the one as to whether singing in the "new or rulable way" or singing in the " usual way " should be encouraged. By singing in the usual way was meant the singing of a few well-known tunes only, supposedly according to usage (although there was none) and without the adventitious help of notes, or, rather, regardless of any enforced uniformity in melody and rhythm. Singing in the new way involved the singing of the old tunes as set down in musical notation and the learning of new ones. The latter, it was freely claimed, would inevitably lead to Quakerism, Popery, and to the introduction into divine service of instrumental music, which was held to be the invention of the Evil One. A new tune could be adopted only after grave consideration of the matter by the church or even the entire parish.

According to contemporaneous testimony the consequences of singing in the usual way, as practised as late as the eighteenth century, were appalling. It appears not to have been exceptional for the congregation to sing parts of two or three different tunes to one stanza of a hymn, even to sing different tunes at the same time. So slowly were these medleys sung that it was often necessary to take breath twice on one and the same tone and word-syllable.

The champions of the new way finally prevailed and also succeeded in silencing the objections which were urged against the establishment of the singing schools indispensable to the carrying out of the innovation. Gradually, though not without much opposition, it was even agreed upon that those who frequented the schools might sit together, and thus church choirs were formed. The fears of those who anticipated the introduction of instruments with the adoption of the new way were now realised. As the duty of giving the pitch could no longer be left to the momentary inspiration of the minister or deacon, the hymns being set for several parts, it was henceforth intrusted to the leader of the choir, and he, depending on a pitch-pipe—generally a large wooden one, not unlike a mouse-trap in appearance — brought the dreaded instrument into the church, as surreptitiously as possible, however. The pitch-pipe was followed in due time by the bass-viol and other stringed instruments and wind instruments. The first organ in Boston, presented to Queen's Chapel in 1713, was permitted, after much wrangling, to be set up in 1714.

With the singing school, which became universal after the second decade of the eighteenth century, the psalm-tune teacher, a type unique in the history of music in America, made his appearance. The original psalm-tune teacher was a religious enthusiast who, endowed with a voice, generally tenor, of more than ordinary sweetness, with more than average musical intelligence, and with an engaging manner, became by natural selection a leader. His principal aim and object was to devise and put into execution a practical method of choral instruction, regardless of the rules of musical theory, of the knowledge of which he was, as a rule, entirely innocent. His life was a peripatetic one, for during the winter months he rode from one town of his circuit to the other, satisfied with a small remuneration besides board for himself and horse, in providing which the patrons of the school alternated. His repertory was confined to hymn tunes and the current anthems. He was the natural ally of the psalm-tune composer and publisher, both of whom were largely dependent on him for the popularity of their newly issued compilations.

The first psalm-tune composer who gained fame, and, indeed, the first American composer, speaking euphemistically, was William Billings (1746–1800), a native of Boston and a tanner by trade. Impelled by his natural musical temperament, he tried his hand at harmonising, then at composing, and in 1770 published his first collection of compositions consisting of psalm tunes, anthems, and canons. Encouraged by the reception of this book, he was inspired to new attempts, and when the Revolutionary War broke out, added to his popularity by his patriotic songs.

Billings was unquestionably a man of unusual musical endowments. He was entirely self-taught, and as his means for acquiring knowledge were very limited — good theoretical treatises were rare in America at that time—his attainments were necessarily of the most superficial sort. Yet he had what were in his estimation high ideals. Not satisfied with setting his melodies to simple harmonies, he devoted himself to composing in the so-called "fuguing style," which he had probably observed in English choruses, and which in its novelty and liveliness proved very attractive to singers accustomed to plainly harmonised hymn tunes. Unfamiliar with the rules of harmony and counterpoint, and therefore undaunted by the difficulties of this style, Billings wrote on, though the results often suggest the discant of the twelfth or the organum of the eleventh century; for he had the courage of his convictions, which he defended cleverly with such aphorisms as "Nature is the best Dictator" and "Art is subservient to Genius." Unfortunately, his dicta were widely accepted and followed, for a time at least, in practice.

Billings's personality was such as to attract notice on account of its very ugliness. He was somewhat deformed, one of his arms and one of his legs being slightly withered; he was blind in one eye, possessed of a stentorian voice, and was given to eccentric habits, perhaps intentionally. Yet he possessed the faculty of attracting and impressing people and the authority which makes the leader.

In 1774 Billings established at Stoughton, Massachusetts, the "Sacred Singing School" of forty-eight members: twenty "singers of tenor," of whom thirteen were women, the rest men; eighteen "singers of treble," all women; five "singers of counter;" and five "singers of bass," all men. Out of this grew the Stoughton Musical Society, which was founded on November 7, 1786, and is still in existence. It was probably the first stable association of amateur singers organised in America, and it is a cause for justifiable pride to Americans that it antedated the Singakademie of Berlin by five years. This fact is the more significant because the Stoughton Society was not the result of a sporadic impulse but representative of a strong movement which gained impetus with astonishing rapidity, for, according to the record of Charles C. Perkins, historian of the Handel and Haydn Society of Boston, there were founded: in the same year the Boston Independent Musical Society, which gave a concert at King's Chapel in 1788; in 1804 the Franklin; in 1806 the Salem; in 1807 the Massachusetts Musical; in 1812 the Lock Hospital; and the Norfolk, date not mentioned. On comparing with this the generally accepted record of German amateur vocal societies for the same period, it appears that in 1812 the regularly established amateur choruses in America outnumbered those in Germany by at least one, possibly by two.

While this and other similar comparisons that might be instituted yield results favourable to choral culture in America, such would not be the case were they extended to the quality of the work done. It can be said, without belittling the services rendered to choral music by the early psalm-tune teachers and composers, and without impugning their sincerity of purpose, that what they accomplished was necessarily crude and unfinished, and that the methods and tendencies which they introduced for want of better knowledge, and which have even now not been completely set aside, were shallow and inartistic. An admirable opportunity to judge of the musical culture of that period was afforded by one hundred members of the Stoughton Society when they performed two programmes made up entirely of hymns and anthems by Billings and other pioneer American composers, at the Chicago Columbian Exposition.

Notwithstanding the fact that their systems and products will not bear close inspection, it is remarkable that the early psalm-tune teachers and psalm-tune composers accomplished what they did, when it is borne in mind that their point of departure was that of the most vitiated taste, that they laboured in the face of

the bitterest opposition, and, above all, that
they were thrown entirely on their own resources in the absence of good theoretical treatises and musical literature.

With increasing facilities for intercourse with
the Old World, and with growing prosperity, the
writings of European musical authorities and
the works of Handel and Haydn were more
easily obtainable, while educated and experienced foreign musicians made their homes in
America in numbers, and disseminated maturer ideas of musical instruction. The effect of
these new conditions was illustrated by the establishment, at Boston, in 1815, of the society
which rendered incalculable service to the
cause of choral culture in America, and which,
from its very inception, testified to the loftiness
of its aims by adopting the name of "The
Handel and Haydn Society." It became to
America what the Singakademie of Berlin was
to Europe—the institution which served as a
model for amateur choral organisations its native country over.

The direct impulse for the foundation of this
society seems to have been given by a series of
musical celebrations in which public enthusiasm over the treaty of peace signed at Ghent
on December 24, 1814, sought vent at Boston.
These culminated in a Peace Jubilee, held the

year following on Washington's birthday, in which a chorus of two hundred and fifty and an orchestra of fifty participated, and which attracted unusual attention and focussed the diffused interest in choral performances. As a result an invitation was issued on March 24, 1815, by a number of music-lovers, to consider " the expediency and practicability of forming a society to consist of a selection from the several choirs, for cultivating and improving a correct taste in the performance of sacred music, and also to introduce into more general practice the works of Handel, Haydn, and other eminent composers." Accordingly, " The Handel and Haydn Society," the name which had been decided upon beforehand, was organised on Thursday morning, April 20th, a constitution adopted and signed by thirty-one gentlemen, and a board of government chosen with Thomas S. Webb as president.

On Christmas-day of the same year the first public concert of the society took place, its programme consisting of the first part of Haydn's " Creation " and selections from Handel's works. The chorus numbered ninety men and ten women, the orchestra about twelve pieces, assisted by an organ. There were nine hundred and forty-five persons in the audience, and the amount realised from the sale of tickets was five hundred and thirty-three dollars. On Christmas-day, 1818, the society for the first time devoted an entire concert to a single work: " The Messiah."

Notwithstanding the encomiums which were lavished on the performances of the Handel and Haydn Society at the time, it is improbable that during the early years of its existence they attained to any degree of artistic excellence. While women were not entirely prevented by prejudice of long standing from singing in the chorus, they participated to a limited extent only, and, above all, hesitated to "lead," as carrying the soprano was called. At best a few joined the men practised in the use of the falsetto and the small number of boys sufficiently trained to be serviceable in taking the soprano part. The English custom of giving the alto part to counter-tenors was followed as a matter of course.

In 1817 the chorus of the society consisted of one hundred and thirty men and boys, who sang all the four parts, and of only twenty women, who assisted the tenors mainly. In the same year the advisability of officially inviting women to lend their help at rehearsals and concerts was favourably considered, though not without opposition. The result of this step was at first harmful, as the women were assigned to the tenor part, which they naturally sang an octave too high, thereby creating the most excruciating harmonic progressions. Yet this method, according to the testimony of Mr. Perkins, held good until Dr. Lowell Mason (1792–1872), who accepted the presidency of the society in 1827, insisted on the proper distribution of the voices.

Until 1847, when the first conductor was elected in the person of Charles E. Horn (1786–1849), an English opera singer and composer, the presidents, with few exceptions amateurs, officiated in that capacity. At the concerts their duty consisted principally in occupying the conductor's stand or box, not unlike a pulpit, the responsibility of leading being assumed by the principal violinist of the orchestra.

It is evident that under such circumstances the attainment of artistic results was out of the question. Indeed, it is difficult to understand how oratorios by Handel and Haydn could have been attempted at all. Yet these efforts created on the part of the singers a desire to study, and on the part of the public a desire to hear a high class of choral works, so that when professional musicians educated in European institutions and versed in European methods drifted to America in numbers, they found conditions favourable to the exercise of their best powers, and were enabled in a comparatively short time to establish loftier standards. In 1852 no less versatile a musician than Carl Bergmann (1821–1876), afterward conductor of the New York Philharmonic Society, assumed the leadership of the Handel and Haydn Society, and two years later Carl Zerrahn (1826–) was intrusted with its musical destinies, which he guided with conspicuous success for forty-one years. To him is due much of the credit of having hastened the promotion of choral culture in America, to which the Handel and Haydn Society of Boston is entitled.

In New York choral culture proceeded on lines independent of those followed in New England. Under the Dutch régime there was nothing to hope from the Church in the way of musical effort. The Dutch Reformed Church was as firmly opposed to the slightest departure from established usage as were the Puritans. Yet of such a bitter controversy as was carried on in New England and of such a type of choral activity as there grew up under it, only faint traces are to be found in New York. Not until the Anglican Church through its authorised representative, Trinity Church, incorporated in 1693, had become a religious and social power, did interest in chorus singing publicly manifest itself.

CARL ZERRAHN.

Trinity Church was supplied with organists and choristers from England. While these were undoubtedly under the spell of the operatic style cultivated in the churches of the parent country after the Restoration, they entertained much maturer ideas concerning music in general and chorus singing in particular than were current at the time in New England.

Dr. Frédéric Louis Ritter (1834–1891), in "Music in America," makes the statement, without, however, mentioning on what authority, that "The Messiah" was performed in Trinity Church with organ accompaniment on January 9, 1770, and repeated on October 3d of the year following, and in April, 1772. While these performances, if they really took place, were in all probability in the nature of special services only and were given by the choristers of Trinity aided by a few amateurs interested in the work, they bear eloquent testimony to the progressive spirit of the choir of Trinity and undoubtedly attracted attention to the oratorio, which was so influential in furthering the cause of choral culture in England at the time.

The oldest reliable records of choral societies in New York go back to the third decade of this century only. That such societies existed before that time admits of little doubt, for the records referred to in speaking of public choral performances do not mention them as of unusual occurrence. Like the organisations regarding which definite information is obtainable, the earlier ones, too, probably had their inception in Episcopal Church choirs, which were required by the nature of their duties to be efficient. The Handel and Haydn Society of New York,—its name was evidently suggested by that of the then firmly established Handel and Haydn Society of Boston—which was the result of a movement to give a concert for the purpose of providing funds to rebuild Zion Church, appears not to have survived long. Its place was taken by two organisations: the New York Choral Society and the New York Sacred Music Society, both of which took shape in 1823. The former, to judge by the programme of its first concert, was at the start the more ambitious and, perhaps for that reason, the more short-lived of the two. This concert took place at St. George's Church, Beekman Street, on April 20, 1824, the choir numbering fifty and the orchestra twenty. Its scheme embraced fourteen numbers, of which ten were by Handel, three of them for chorus. In addition to these the choir sang a motet by Mozart and the " Hallelujah " from Beethoven's " The Mount of Olives," the latter, which was heard for the first time in America on this occasion, with such effect that the audience demanded its repetition. This programme and the enthusiasm which its performance aroused speak well for the early musical taste of the metropolis.

The New York Sacred Music Society, which in a short time came to be considered one of the most efficient choral bodies then existing in America, grew out of the choir of Zion Church, which, having been refused an increase of salary as well as permission to give a concert in lieu of it, severed its connection with the church and continued its activity as an independent body. Its first concert took place in the Presbyterian Church, in Prevost Street, on March 15, 1824. In 1827 the society gave a concert with a chorus of sixty and an orchestra of twenty-seven, which was made memorable by the great Malibran's (1808–1836) singing of " Angels Ever Bright and Fair," and added materially to the choir's prestige. On November 18, 1831, it entered upon its real mission by giving " The Messiah " as the first of the series of oratorio performances which it carried on successfully until 1849.

Although none of the many choral societies which sprang up from time to time had a long career until the Oratorio Society was organised,

the lovers of choral music in New York were
not without opportunities to keep in touch with
the older masterpieces of choral composition
and to become acquainted with the more important new ones. On the grave of one chorus
another was sure to blossom into life. Finally,
in 1873, the agencies and conditions necessary
to the establishment of a choral institution on
a permanent basis were present.

In 1871 Dr. Leopold Damrosch (1832–1885)
was called to New York to assume the direc-
torship of the Arion, a German Maennerchor
the activity of which, like that of most male
choruses, was necessarily circumscribed both
as to artistic possibilities and as to influence on
musical culture at large. Dr. Damrosch's in-
quiries in regard to the opportunities of finding
a wider and more congenial sphere by founding
a society of mixed voices were met with dis-
couraging replies until 1873, when, at the initiative of a lady who had been a member of a
chorus at Cologne conducted by Ferdinand
Hiller (1811–1885), a number of music-lovers
agreed to make the attempt to interest capable
singers in such a project. The use of Trinity
Chapel having been secured for the meetings
of the choir, the first rehearsal was held, fifteen
or twenty persons being present.

The innumerable obstacles which invariably

LEOPOLD DAMROSCH.

confront such an organisation were overcome
with the aid of the devotion of the singers and
the self-sacrificing efforts of the business admin-
istration, which the high aims, the zeal, and the
infectious enthusiasm of the conductor, who,
as Fasch in Berlin had done, lent his services
without any remuneration, did not permit to lag
for a moment. The first entertainment, given
by the new society on December 3, 1873, with
a chorus of between fifty and sixty, forecast the
lofty purpose of the organisation and its conductor. The programme was made up principally
of choral works by Palestrina, Bach, Handel,
Mozart, and Mendelssohn, and its performance
called forth many tributes of acknowledgment
and enlisted the co-operation of new members.
The expectations of arousing public interest in
the organisation were modest indeed. Mr. H.
E. Krehbiel relates in his admirable monograph
" Notes on Choral Music," from which the facts
relating to the Oratorio Society are gleaned,
that as no public announcement of the second
concert had been made, no measures for the
sale of tickets of admission at the door had been
taken, and that the business management was
much surprised when the necessity of such
measures was made apparent on the evening
of the performance by the crowd's waiting to
purchase tickets. A box-office was hastily im-

provised and between twenty and twenty-five dollars added to the society's funds.

With the third concert, which took place in Steinway Hall, on May 12, 1874, the Oratorio Society, still numbering less than a hundred singers, entered upon the field in which it has since remained conspicuously active, by the successful production with full orchestral accompaniment of Handel's " Samson." The chorus gradually grew in numbers and efficiency and placed to its credit performances—not a few of them notable ones—of the classical oratorios and cantatas which make up the standard repertory of such fully equipped choral institutions, as well as of works of the modern school of composition. The fact that the Oratorio Society is still in full vigour, while numerous efforts to found similar organisations in New York have been only temporarily successful, affords eloquent proof of the earnest spirit which was infused from the very beginning into its active members, and of the wisdom with which its administrative system was framed.

It was principally under the influence emanating from the singing schools of New England and spread abroad by New England singing school teachers and their disciples that choral culture in its rudimentary form found its way into other sections of the country. The extent to which it was subsequently developed depended on local conditions and upon the capability and seriousness of purpose of those who assumed the duty of directing it. In the course of time, by the process of natural selection, centres were formed about which the musical activity of certain sections revolved.

In the West, Cincinnati became such a centre. As early as 1800—Cincinnati was founded in 1788 and incorporated as a city in 1814—it boasted of a singing school, and in a call for subscriptions to " The Western Harmonist," issued in 1815, the existence of singing societies is referred to. A choral society was founded in 1816, and there is record of a concert given three years later by the Haydn Society, in which choruses from oratorios by Handel and Haydn were sung. From that time on choral activity, though fluctuating, gathered impetus until with the first May Festival, held in 1873, it assumed proportions and accomplished results which deservedly attracted the attention of the whole country.

The German population of Cincinnati was noted for its efforts to promote the cultivation of the German part-song. It was at Cincinnati that the first Sängerfest in America was held in 1849, only four years after such reunions had been introduced in Germany at

Würzburg; and it was the Sängerfest of 1870, in which two thousand singers took part and for which a special building was erected, that suggested the idea of arranging a similar festival with the aid of the mixed choruses of Cincinnati and the adjacent towns. In the spring of 1872 the plan was broached to Theodore Thomas (1835–), who was at the time making a tour through the West with his orchestra. He entered heartily into the project, insisting, however, on the elimination of the festive features so indispensable to the Sängerfest scheme. Accordingly, the first Cincinnati Music Festival took place from May 6 to May 9, 1873, under the direction of Mr. Thomas, thirty-six societies, aggregating one thousand and eighty-three singers, of whom six hundred and forty were residents of Cincinnati, participating. The orchestra numbered one hundred and eight pieces. In the course of subsequent festivals the assistance of outside choral contingents was dispensed with, and in 1880 the local festival chorus, the membership of which has since fluctuated between three and six hundred, was organised.

The record of the Cincinnati Music Festivals —they have taken place biennially with one exception — is a proud one and a monument to the genius and artistic conscientiousness of

Mr. Thomas, to the faithfulness of the chorus singers of the city, and to the public spirit of its inhabitants.

Among other permanently organised choirs in the West, the influence of which has extended beyond their immediate environments, the Apollo Club of Chicago, founded in 1872 as a male chorus and converted four years later into a society of mixed voices by W. L. Tomlins, has assumed a leading position.

Of long standing are many of the German organisations to be found throughout this country. They devote themselves almost exclusively to the study of part-songs for male voices and, being invariably connected with institutions social in character, do not often appear in public. Most of the German mixed choirs, of which there are a number of efficient ones, are governed by the same circumstances. Notwithstanding their exclusiveness, these societies contributed their share towards stimulating the practice of choral music, especially in the West, at a time when chorus singing was in its infancy there. That one or the other of them steadfastly held in view the loftiest aims was illustrated when on March 27th of last year the Bach choir of Bethlehem, Penn., consisting of about one hundred singers, produced complete for the first time in America Bach's stupendous mass in B minor. This choir represented the result of the musical activity which was begun in that place by the Moravians in the shape of a Collegium Musicum probably more than a century ago.

Of recent years the singing of part-songs for men's voices has been very generally taken up by Americans and with such earnestness that, so far as technical perfection is concerned, excellent results have been achieved. It is to its mixed choral societies, however, that a community must look for the diffusion of sound musical taste. Although these have steadily increased in number and capability, the benefit to be derived from the opportunities which they offer for participating in the practice and listening to the performance of choral works of a high class is but little appreciated. Good choruses are not numerous because the dignity and educational value of chorus singing are not understood. Few, even of the best organisations, enter upon a new season confident of the public support necessary to their very life. Much less are they in the position to pursue a course in accord with the lofty ideals which they may have in view regardless of popular prejudice. In the whole range of choral literature there is but one work the performance of which, if given about Christmastide, can be relied upon for liberal patronage. That work is " The Messiah," and its production is looked upon as a religious function. Under such conditions it is impossible to adopt a policy calculated systematically to develop the technical capabilities and powers of comprehension of the chorus and to educate the taste of the public.

It was largely the necessity of employing adventitious means to attract the public that called into life the musical festivals, so called, which of recent years have become common in the smaller towns and rely in a great measure on the drawing power of vocal celebrities for their pecuniary success. With all their obvious disadvantages and their inconsistencies as educational institutions, these festivals have the merit at least of making it possible occasionally to provide orchestral accompaniment and capable soloists for the performance of the choral works mastered after months of labour—a luxury not ordinarily within reach of societies remote from the musical centres. While the larger number of festivals have been planned with this end in view, some of them, such as those occurring annually at Worcester, Mass., had their origin in conventions organised by the psalm-tune teachers for the improvement of church music.

Events of extraordinary magnitude yet of artistic dignity were the musical festivals given in 1881 at New York under the direction of Dr. Leopold Damrosch with a chorus of twelve hundred and an orchestra of two hundred and fifty; and the one which took place in the same city the year following under the direction of Mr. Theodore Thomas, when the chorus, made up of societies from New York, Boston, Philadelphia, Worcester, Baltimore, and Reading, numbered three thousand, and the orchestra three hundred and two.

Almost entirely neglected in this country is the study of unaccompanied choral music for mixed voices and the study of the works of the mediæval composers in particular. Yet this is the most effective means for the certain attain. ment of the qualities upon which good chorus singing depends, and should be cultivated if for no other purpose than that of raising the standard of choral technics. The prevailing tendency in musical taste is distinctly unfavourable to the appreciation of choral works in the polyphonic style. These appeal to the heart and to the emotions through the intellect. Their beauty and grandeur lie largely in the consistency and symmetry of their structure, which can be comprehended only by the exercise of musical faculties trained to look beyond nerve excitation for the content of a composition. Such training is not encouraged by the preponderance of descriptive, picturesque, and dramatic music, which acts more directly upon the senses, although here, too, the employment of analytical capability can prove advantageous only, while to the acquirement of clear judgment and sound taste it is indispensable. To form the habit of discriminate listening and to assist in spreading it, are the loftiest privileges and duties of the members of properly conducted singing societies. With understanding will develop love for the highest types of choral music, and with love, the support necessary to the existence of choral institutions.

X

The Chorus and the Chorus Conductor

CHORUS singing as an independent art
reached its culmination in the achieve-
ment of the mediæval professional choirs which
devoted themselves to the interpretation of the
unaccompanied works of the Palestrina school.
These relied for their proper effect on beauty
of tone quality, absolute purity of intonation,
and faultless vocalisation. As soon as instrumental music encroached on the domain of vocal music, and forcefulness of expression became
paramount to considerations of sensuous beauty, composers began to show their disregard
for the nature of the human voice by assigning to it tone progressions foreign to its idiosyncrasies, and by compelling it to adapt itself
to the instrumental vernacular. Harsh disso-
nances took the place of mellow consonances,
for the production of which the human voice is
fitted as no other tonal medium, while the instrumental support, as it helped the voices to
execute unmelodic tone successions, made sing-

ers less solicitous of the beauty of quality, perfection of intonation, and delicacy of tone modulation which were the fundamental requirements of the unaccompanied polyphonic style.

All this was in line with the growing demand for emotional power and dramatic expression in music. The time for looking upon sensuous beauty as the one indispensable element of music had passed, and with it the time for cultivating chorus singing for the sake of its own peculiar tonal charm. The subdivision of the chorus into a large number of independent voice parts for the purpose of having at hand many strands for the intricate polyphonic texture and means for the production of a variety of vocal tone colours, fell into disuse, and in its stead the more compact scheme of four parts became the normal one. With greater sonorousness in the orchestral accompaniment a corresponding increase in the vocal tone volume became imperative, and this called for larger numbers of choristers. Under the influence of dramatic music choral forms grew up unsuited to the ritual of the Church, and with these the church singers could concern themselves to a limited extent only. The oratorio in particular began to attract attention as a substitute for the all-absorbing opera. Thus step by step chorus singing, which for centuries had been intrusted to professional church choristers only, was brought within the scope and sphere of amateur activity, and one of the most efficient means for the propagation of musical culture was placed within the reach of the people.

That chorus singing as an art suffered thereby is undeniable. The refinements which were the common property of mediæval choristers are all but lost. That they are not dominating factors in the interpretation of modern accompanied and, to a certain extent, of modern unaccompanied choral music, does not alter this fact. Amateur choral culture, however, is in its infancy as yet, and the time may come when it will arrive at a stage of development which will make it possible to revive the taste for so pure and lofty a style of unaccompanied chorus music as is that of the mediæval church composers. In the meanwhile singing societies are fulfilling a high mission in diffusing love for music, not only by providing the public with opportunities for becoming acquainted with such choral literature as they can undertake to perform, but also by creating in their members that sincere affection for a dignified type of music which is borne of the thorough knowledge attainable only by unremitting study.

The Chorus and the Chorus Conductor

Were the benefits to be derived in every direction from singing in a properly directed chorus fully appreciated, the organisation of efficient amateur societies would be a much easier matter than it is. Instead of such appreciation the idea is prevalent that choral practice is harmful in many ways. The following remarks on this subject by Dr. H. Kretzschmar, until very recently the conductor of one of the most celebrated choirs in Germany, the Riedel Society of Leipsic, and an acknowledged authority on choral culture, are to the point :—

That by such [amateur] societies harm should be wrought to the art of singing, that with them artistically perfect results cannot be achieved, only those can assert that know little about the matter. Everything depends upon the question as to who stands at the head and how the rehearsals are conducted. Wherever one piece after the other is disposed of with the aid of piano thumping, singing must soon come to an end. The training, or at least the supervision of the individual member must form the foundation of choral activity, and the performance and study of accompanied compositions must constitute only half of the work. Constant practice in *a cappella* singing is indispensable. It is this that trains the ear and teaches vocalisation just as well as, if not better than the study of solos in which half the faults are hidden and half the trouble saved for the less gifted by the piano. . . . A choral society which now and then sings a few movements by Palestrina or a fine madrigal will give a more beautiful performance of a Handel oratorio than one whose sense for tone has not been independently awakened.

The opinion that the gifts and attainments necessary to an efficient chorus singer are of an inferior kind is another fallacy commonly entertained, particularly by those who aspire to recognition of their individual talents. Yet it is none the less true that there is the widest scope in chorus singing for the exercise of the highest musical qualities. A member of a choral body, so it be capable of artistic work, must have a good voice, properly trained; an ear sensitive to the slightest deviation from the true pitch; keen perceptiveness of rhythm; a systematically developed faculty for reading music; and an artistic temperament. He must be self-reliant, but not self-assertive, patient, eager to learn, filled with love for his task, and appreciative of the benefit to be derived for musical intelligence and taste from the concerted practice of the works of the great choral masters; for no amount of individual application can give such insight into the deeper meaning of a composition as does the earnest participation in chorus rehearsals in which every phrase of a complicated musical structure is repeatedly laid bare before the work is presented in its entirety to the spiritual ear. Part of a grand aggregate though he be, the singer will find in choral activity ample opportunity not only to make use of all the technical resources which he may have acquired by years of study, but to develop them and apply them to a higher purpose than that of mere self-aggrandisement. No more effective means for the correction of vocal vices and aberrations of taste can be found than the study of dignified choral works under the guidance of a competent and exacting conductor.

One of the most serious rudimentary shortcomings of amateur choruses consists in the lack of balance between the different parts. Due generally to the scarcity of voices of one or another class, most frequently of tenors, its only remedy lies in taking the weakest part as the basis of adjustment. Were this more strenuously carried out, amateur singing societies would be much smaller but much more capable of attaining good results than they are as a rule.

Given a well-balanced body of such singers as have been described, it remains for the conductor to secure beauty of tone quality throughout all gradations of force, purity of intonation, accuracy and elasticity of rhythm, correct phrasing, clear enunciation, truthful expression, and characteristic declamation.

The antiquity of the office of the chorus conductor is indicated by what has been said in a former chapter regarding the Hebrew, Greek, and Roman chorus leaders. In the Christian Church, the principal arena for artistic activity up to the seventeenth century, the need of a conductor must have become apparent as early as the fourth century, when trained choirs were instituted. It is safe to assume that a fixed system of leading was introduced as soon as detailed instructions for the performance of the music of the ritual were dictated by the ecclesiastical authorities. These instructions prescribed not only the melodies for all the services, but the precise way in which they should be sung and fitted to the ceremonies. In order to accommodate the different melodic phrases with their dynamic gradations to the movements of the celebrants at the altar, it was necessary to accelerate or retard the speed with the utmost nicety, and it is evident that the singers could not make these changes without the ruling hand of a conductor. From the few scattered references to the subject obtainable, it appears that the conductor conveyed his intention to the singer by means of the " sólfa," a roll of parchment or paper, or a stick of wood, with which he executed motions suggestive of the constantly changing rhythm and nuances of the chants—that he sketched out the melody, as it were, with gestures before the eyes of the choir—and that this art was considered very difficult of attainment. After the introduction of measured music the method which is known to have been in vogue ever since the fifteenth century in the Sistine Chapel, the direct descendant of the early Roman singing school, was probably adopted. It consisted in the conductor's beating the time with the sólfa visibly to the choir and frequently audibly to all within hearing. In so doing he indicated the units of measurement only by the up and down motion, just as the Greek coryphæi had done two thousand years before, with whom, however, the up-beat, which now represents the unaccented unit, represented the accented one. As the music was not divided into measures, this method, which is still in use in the churches of Italy remaining faithful to the mediæval ecclesiastical style, was sufficiently accurate.

When in dramatic music the harpsichord was introduced for the accompaniment of the "dry recitative" (the recitative supported by detached chords only), conductors availed themselves of that instrument on account of its soft but crisp tone, to control their forces, resorting when necessary to gestures. This custom found its way into the churches which permitted accompanied music. At concerts on an elaborate scale two harpsichords were frequently employed, one by the conductor and the other by the accompanist. Nevertheless the sólfa or baton, as it is now called, re-

mained in use, while in France the habit of
marking the time by striking the floor with the
end of a cane was not uncommon. Samuel
Pepys (1633–1703), the entertaining English di-
arist, relates that he heard music at the Globe
and saw "the simple motion that is there of
a woman with a rod in her hand keeping time
to the music while it plays; which is simple
methinks;" and Dr. Burney, who in his enthusiasm over the Handel Commemoration took
occasion to praise everything connected with
that event, even the tuning of the orchestra,
referred to the absence of a time-beating conductor in the following words:

Foreigners, particularly the French, must be much as-
tonished at so numerous a band moving in exact measure
without the assistance of a *coryphæus* to beat the time either
with a roll of paper or a noisy *baton* or truncheon. Lulli
may be said to have *beat himself to death* by intemperate
passion in marking the measure to an ill-disciplined band,
for in regulating with his cane the time of a Te Deum in
1686, he wounded his foot by accidentally striking on that
instead of the floor; from the contusion a mortification en-
sued which cost him his life at the age of fifty-four. This
commemoration is the first instance of *any band* at all numerous performing in a similar situation without the assistance of a manuductor.

Choruses as now constituted and prepared
for concerts would scarcely be equal to such
an undertaking. Yet how much is to be ac-

complished by faithful study was shown at the performance of Bach's B minor mass at Bethlehem, already mentioned, which was directed, as in Bach's days, by the organist from the organ-bench. None the less the present method of accustoming the chorus to rely implicitly on the conductor by paying the closest possible heed to his every gesture and signal is unquestionably the one which can be made to yield the best results.

The view is all too prevalent that the conductor of amateur singing societies need not be a musician of such high endowments, comprehensive knowledge, and thorough technical training as the conductor of a body of professional performers; yet the influence of the former for good or evil is much more far-reaching than that of the latter. Not only are the teachings of the chorus conductor more widely disseminated, but they are more unreservedly appropriated and more perfectly assimilated because amateurs are more numerous and susceptible and are compelled by the very nature of choral training to submit to these teachings so constantly that they cannot but make them their own. The power of the chorus conductor, therefore, to elevate or debase musical taste is unlimited. As choral music embraces a great diversity of styles and types, it is incumbent on every conductor of singing societies, however brilliant his gifts may be, to devote the most careful and conscientious study to the master works of all periods in order to acquire standards of judgment which are in accord with recognised art canons and well-authenticated traditions. Without such standards it is impossible to arrive at the correct conception of the choral music of the mediæval masters and even of Bach and his contemporaries, which is not at all, or very sparingly provided with the clews to interpretation now liberally supplied; nor are such standards unnecessary to the full appreciation of the modern classic and romantic composers.

In respect of the technique of training singers the chorus leader must be well equipped. He must possess keen musical faculties, thoroughly developed; exhaustive theoretical and practical knowledge of conducting; intimate familiarity with the nature and the management of the human voice, and with the effects peculiar to chorus singing and to the combination of voices and instruments, not to speak of the subtler personal gifts and accomplishments requisite to the government and instruction of singers in whom loving interest in their work must be awakened and sustained.

Among the many perplexing questions which

The Chorus and the Chorus Conductor

the conductor of choral societies is called upon
to solve is that of the interrelation of the chorus and the orchestra. In works of the modern
school, in which the orchestra is used not only
to reinforce the chorus but as an independent
means of illustration and expression, frequently
in protracted instrumental movements, a body
of not less than sixty instrumentalists—the number necessary to the full symphony orchestra
so its constituent elements be well balanced—
is required. It remains for the conductor to
adjust the tone volume of such an orchestra to
that of his chorus, and in so doing he must be
guided by his appreciation of the character of
the work to be performed, and by his conception of the nature of its several movements,
each of which may demand a different treatment. The increase in the size of choirs since
choral performances have been taken in hand
by amateurs has not been accompanied with a
corresponding increase in tone volume. The
numerical relation between the orchestral and
choral forces which was observed when choruses were made up of professionals, has been
reversed not so much on account of the greater
sonority of modern instrumentation as on account of the decline in the effectiveness of chorus singing, unavoidable under the conditions
which as yet govern amateur activity. In il-

lustration of the comparative effect produced
by a body of selected, perfectly trained, and
one of ordinary, indifferently trained voices,
it may be stated that at the coronation of Napoleon I. in the Cathedral of Notre Dame,
Paris, the singing of the thirty-two choristers
of the Papal chapel created a more profound
impression than that of a chorus of hundreds
of voices accompanied by eighty harps, which
had been gathered together for the occasion.

In the opinion of Berlioz modern orchestration does not necessitate a radical readjustment
of the numerical relation between singers and
players considered normal at the time of Bach
and Handel, provided the former be as capable individually and collectively as the latter.
Berlioz, whose judgment in such matters can
be unreservedly accepted, held that to a hall of
the size of that of the Conservatoire, which con-
tains, in round numbers, one thousand seats, an
orchestra of one hundred and nineteen and a
chorus of one hundred and twenty-six would be
perfectly adapted, and that for a musical festival in an acoustically well-constructed building,
four hundred and sixty-seven instrumentalists
and three hundred and sixty chorus singers, including forty boy sopranos, would be required,
an additional chorus of boys' voices to be at
hand when needed. The quality of the chorus

singers he had in mind he defined by adding
that great difficulty would be experienced in
collecting in Paris such a number of voices of
any excellence. Berlioz's Te Deum was produced in the church of St. Eustache in 1855 on
about the scale indicated by these figures, nine
hundred executants participating. The model
concerts given at the Paris Conservatoire enlisted during the past year the co-operation of
an orchestra of eighty-six and a chorus of only
seventy-four, divided into nineteen sopranos,
eighteen contraltos, eighteen tenors, and nineteen basses. On the other hand, at the concerts of the Philharmonic Chorus of Berlin, one
of the most efficient amateur organisations on
the Continent, the orchestra during the past
season numbered about seventy and the chorus four hundred and three : one hundred and
sixty-two sopranos, one hundred and thirty-one
contraltos, forty-eight tenors, and sixty-two
basses; while at the Cincinnati Music Festival
of 1898 an orchestra of one hundred and nine
was associated with a chorus of four hundred
and thirty-nine (not including a choir of one
hundred and twenty-six boys required for the
closing number of Berlioz's " Damnation of
Faust"), divided into one hundred and forty-
six sopranos, one hundred and thirty-two contraltos, fifty-seven tenors, and one hundred and

four basses. These figures show how remarkable are the numerical discrepancies to which amateur culture has given rise and the difficulties which the conductor of non-professional choruses is called upon to meet in order to bring about artistic results.

The solution of the problem of placing the choir and orchestra in such a way as to enable each body to develop its full power, and both bodies in conjunction to produce a homogeneous tone quality, involves the careful consideration of the acoustic properties of the halls available, most of which, especially in this country, are constructed with the requirements of dramatic representations in view and are therefore ill adapted to concert performances. Under such circumstances the conductor will resort to the devices which his knowledge and experience may suggest. Under normal conditions the seating plan usually adopted for the chorus consists in placing the singers in converging straight, or in semi-circular rows, each row being sufficiently elevated above the one immediately in advance to permit of its being in unobstructed view of the conductor and the audience. The sopranos are generally seated at the left of the conductor, with the tenors behind them and the altos at the right, with the basses in the rear. Modifications of this plan

may be advisable in order to make compensation for the weakness of a particular part. For
the purpose of assuring a more perfect amalga-
mation of the different voice parts Rubinstein
advocated the subdivision of the chorus into
two sections, each one complete in itself, to be
placed respectively at the right and at the left
of the conductor, whether the composition to
be performed require a double chorus or not.
He even urged a similar disposition of the
strings of the orchestra. In works in which
the orchestral accompaniment serves principally to support the chorus the seating plan offers
little difficulty. When, however, as is the case in
most modern compositions, all the tone colours
attainable by the most advanced methods of instrumentation are to be brought out independently of the vocal part as well as in connection
with it, the question as to how the integrity of
the instrumental body is to be preserved without sacrificing that of the vocal one is not so
easily determined. When the chorus is small,
and so well trained as to give out a refined and
perfectly homogeneous tone body, it can be ad-
vantageously stationed in front of the orchestra,
the seating plan of which remains undisturbed.
This is the course adopted at the Paris Conservatoire, the sopranos and altos being placed
at the left and the tenors and basses at the right

227

of the conductor. For obvious reasons this plan is not practicable when the vocalists outnumber the instrumentalists four or five to one. Under such circumstances it is customary to place the orchestra in front of and into the semicircle formed by the chorus, or to extend it into the chorus ranks in the shape of a triangle with its apex towards the conductor. The latter scheme, which is observed at the concerts of the Berlin Philharmonic Chorus, is illustrated by the following diagram, kindly furnished by the conductor of that society, Prof. Siegfried Ochs:

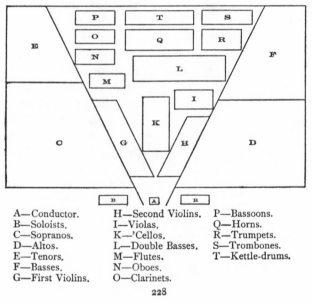

A—Conductor.
B—Soloists.
C—Sopranos.
D—Altos.
E—Tenors.
F—Basses.
G—First Violins.
H—Second Violins.
I—Violas.
K—'Cellos.
L—Double Basses.
M—Flutes.
N—Oboes.
O—Clarinets.
P—Bassoons.
Q—Horns.
R—Trumpets.
S—Trombones.
T—Kettle-drums.

The Chorus and the Chorus Conductor

Unique was the system on which Verdi arranged his forces when he directed a performance of his Requiem at Vienna. He placed all the executants in a complete circle round about him, and, it is said, to the evident advantage of musical effect.

In what way the influences emanating from the modern lyric drama, which are making themselves felt in every sphere of musical composition, will ultimately affect the forms of choral music, the methods of choral writing, and, in consequence, chorus singing itself, it is impossible to forecast. That the scope of choral technics should be extended in various directions and new difficulties be presented to singers is inevitable. In the meantime choral culture, which is now almost exclusively in charge of amateurs, has not yet outgrown the requirements of existing choral literature, nor has musical understanding risen above its appreciation. There are untold treasures of chorus music, accompanied and unaccompanied, of which singing societies are as ignorant as the public. It cannot be too often repeated that to study and listen to the performance of polyphonic works of the highest type afford the surest and quickest means of developing musical intelligence. Inability to realise the dignity and loftiness of such works is a proof of narrowness and want of discrimination, not an evidence of advanced taste. To be so steeped in admiration for glowing tone colour as to be incapable of enjoying the beauty of structural perfection is an indication of unsound taste. He who has learned to understand Bach and Handel will comprehend Wagner much more fully than he whose horizon is limited by Wagner and his followers. Those communities which have supported and continue to support choral societies guided by high purposes are in the possession of the most efficient agencies for the dissemination of genuine and intelligent love for music. No plea for the encouragement and promotion of choral culture can be strong enough.

INDEX

Index

Index

Index

Index

235

Index

Index

Index

Index

Index

Index

Index

Index

Mason, Dr. Lowell, 197

Mass, the, 154 *et seq.*

Masses, Bach's, in B minor, 154, 207 *et seq.*; Haydn's and Mozart's, 154 *et seq.*; Beethoven's, in D, 155 *et seq.*

Massachusetts Musical Society, the, 192

Measured music, 48 *et seq.*; metrical system of, 53

Mediæval composers, 29

Medici, at Florence, 60

Medius, 45

Melodic style, the, in the sacred drama, 117

Melodic turns, conventional, 45 *et seq.*

Melodrama, Greek, 12

Melody, independence of, demonstrated, 34

Members of singing societies, associate, 89

Men's voices, in Hebrew choruses, 4, 7; in Greek choruses, 13; in the early Christian Church, 45; in select choirs, 54; *vide* falsetto singing, counter-tenors, and male altos

Mendelssohn, 98, 182, 145 *et seq.*; compared with Bach and Handel, 145; his style, 145; his mastery of choral forms, 146 *et seq.*; overrated, 146; underrated, 146; his skill in improvisation, 51; his influence in England, 151

Mendelssohn, Fanny, 148

" Messiah, The," Handel's, 127, 128, 140, 180, 182, 196, 201, 209; epic form of, 129; dramatic

conception of, 129 *et seq.*; analysis of, 130; history of, 131; first performance of, 131 *et seq.*; in London, 133; performances of, during Handel's lifetime, 133; popularity of, 134; at Berlin, 135 *et seq.*; attempts to modernize, 135 *et seq.*; in Boston, 196; in New York, 199; attractive power of, 208 *et seq.*

Metre, duple and triple in the twelfth century, 48; intricacies of, 53

Metrical construction of German chorales, 81

Mi, 40, 42

Michael Angelo, 64

Milow, 167

Miracle plays, the, 78, 114; their deterioration, 115 *et seq.*

Modern music, source of, 20

Modes, Greek, 27; authentic, 27; plagal, 28; ecclesiastical, 42, 62

Monastic schools, 32; in England, 67; in Germany, 83; dramatic performances in, 114

Moralities, the, 96, 115

Moravians, the, 208

Mos palatinus, 59

Moses, Song of Moses and Miriam, 4 *et seq.*

" Moses's Song," Handel's, 129

" Moses," Rubinstein's, 151

Motet, the, 52

Motets, hymn texts treated in the form of, 70; Bach's, 110 *et seq.*

Motetus, 45

243

Index

Index

Index

Index

Ratisbon, chorister school of, 78
Ravenscroft, his volume of hymns, 70 ; their character, 70
Re, 40, 42
Recitative, the, in the Passion, 100 ; unaccompanied, 108 ; Handel's, 122
Rectores chori, 89
" Redemption, The," Gounod's, 151
Reformation, the, in England, 69; influence of, on German music, 80
Reforms, musical and liturgical, not due to Gregory, 28
Reichardt, 166
Reichenau, Abbey, band of, 35
Reinstrumentation of Handel's works, 135 *et seq.*
Renaissance, its influence on music, 76
" Representation of the Soul and the Body," Cavaliere's, 117 *et seq.*
Requiem, the, 156
Requiems, Mozart's, 154, 171; Brahms's, 157 ; Verdi's, 157 ; Berlioz's, 157
Restoration, the, hymns after, 70; cathedral chorus after, 75
" Return of Tobias, The," Haydn's, 139
Rhythm, 120 ; of early Christian hymns, 27 ; of chorales, 81
Rhythmic design, not introduced by measured music, 49; due to the folksong, 49
Richter, Hans, 181
Riedel Society of Leipsic, the,

Ripieni, instrumental groups, 126
Ritter, Dr. Frédéric Louis, 199
Roman choristers in England, 67
Roman mysteries, the, 92
Roman pantomimes, 93
Romantic movement, the, its influence on the oratorio, 144
Romanus, 94
Rome, the oratorio in, 117
Rosingrave, Mr., 133
Rossini, 158
Round, the, 72
Roundheads, their war on music, 75
Rubinstein, 151 *et seq.*, 227
Rue, Pierre de la, 53
" Rule, Britannia," 183
Rupf, 80

SACKBUT, the, 77
Sacred Harmonic Society of London, the, 137, 176 *et seq.*, 183
Sacred Music Society, the New York, 200, 201
Sacred operas, the, of Rubinstein, 151 *et seq.*
Sacred Singing School, the, at Stoughton, Mass., 192
" Sacrifice of Abraham, The," 115
Salamonis, Elias, 36 *et seq.*
Salem Society, the, 192
Salieri, 142
" Samson," Handel's, 204
" Sängerfest," 174 ; in Cincinnati, 205
San Girolamo, oratorio of the monastery, 116
" Saul," Handel's, 129

Index

Index

Index

Index